Inaction breeds doubt and fear. Action breeds confidence and courage. If you want to conquer fear, do not sit home and think about it. Go out and get busy.

—Dale Carnegie

DEDICATION

I dedicate this book to my family: my mom, my dad, my brother, my wife, and my children. I love my family and am thankful and grateful to have each of them in my life.

I also dedicate this to the Action Takers: those who read this book and are inspired to do the hard work necessary to fulfill their dreams. For me, there is no better joy than to see people pursue their passions.

Life is too short—go out there and make it happen!

WHY NOT YOU?

**TEN POWERFUL BELIEFS
TO INSPIRE YOU
TO FULFILL YOUR DREAMS**

DARIN BATCHELDER

TZK PRESS

TZK Press

Copyright ©2022 by Darin Batchelder

All rights reserved. No part of this publication may be reproduced, distributed, or transmitted in any form or by any means, including photocopying, recording, or other electronic or mechanical methods, without the prior written permission of the publisher, except in the case of brief quotations embodied in critical reviews and certain other non-commercial uses permitted by copyright law.

Note: This publication is presented solely for informational, educational, and entertainment purposes. It is not intended to provide legal, financial, investment, or other business advice and should not be relied upon as such. If expert assistance is required, the services of a professional should be sought. The publisher and the author and their affiliated entities and individuals do not make any guarantees or other promises as to any results that may be obtained from using the content of this book. To the maximum extent permitted by law, the publisher and the author and their affiliated entities and individuals disclaim any and all liability in the event any information contained in this book proves to be inaccurate, incomplete, or unreliable, or results in any investment or other losses. Further, any laws and regulations referenced in this book may vary from state-to-state and are subject to change. You, the reader, are responsible for your own choices, actions, and results.

Published by TZK Press

Editorial services by GMK Writing and Editing, Inc.
Managing Editor Katie Benoit
Copyedited by Josh Rosenberg
Proofread by Ilana Krebs
Cover design by Libby Kingsbury
Interior design by Libby Kingsbury
Text layout by Sue Murray

Paperback: ISBN: 978-1-7379571-6-4
Ebook: ISBN: 978-1-7379571-7-1

Printed in the United States of America

ACKNOWLEDGMENTS

Wow—where do I start? There are so many people I consider important in my life, so try as I might, I'm sure I'll overlook a few. If your name is among those I unintentionally miss, please forgive me.

First: my wife, Tiffany. She has supported me with each new business idea and life challenge. Writing a book for the first time can feel daunting, and she has always been quick to tell me "you got this." I very much appreciate her love and support.

My children: My son and my daughter are young adults in their late teens / early 20s. I don't know how to explain it but doing something that makes my children proud is a huge blessing.

My mom, my dad, and my brother: Spending time with each of you has formed the foundation for my success, and I'm thankful for all of the love you have poured into my life.

Friends: I realize how fortunate I am to have had so many. Some have encouraged my ventures over the years, while others considered my ideas crazy. I'm thankful for each of them taking the time to listen and pour back into my life—both personally and professionally.

I'm thankful to prior business bosses with whom I've worked over the years. They not only invested in me as an employee but also as a person. I would like to recognize two great people in particular: Vinny Buxo and Paul Forte. Not only did they focus on the bottom line, but they also took the time to invest in others and build leaders.

Multifamily mentor: Brad Sumrok. In the beginning, I didn't know how to go bigger in large-scale multifamily investing. I joined Brad's group in Dallas and was immediately introduced to a community of go-getters who knew how to get these deals done. These individuals were so helpful in terms of teaching me how I could do this myself. I've since met so many wonderful people in this group who have helped further my journey.

Multifamily business partner: I am very thankful to Raj Gupta for partnering with me on my first multifamily syndication property. Raj brought the experience and knowledge that I was lacking. I've learned a great deal from Raj and consider him to be a good friend.

Podcasting: I owe a lot to Chris Krimitsos, the creator

of Podfest. Years ago, I flew down to Orlando, Florida, to my first Podfest conference, where I met so many excellent podcasters who were encouraging and supportive. I also met Juergen Berkessel, founder of Polymash, a consulting firm I hired to help design my website and launch my podcast. Juergen is a pleasure to work with.

This book: I didn't know how to write a book, but I hired Gary M. Krebs, an amazing writer and great guy to work with. I met Gary while attending Dr. Greg S. Reid's Secret Knock conferences. Gary walked me through the entire process. Writing a book can be a project that feels out of reach, but Gary simplified the process to make it much more manageable.

Lastly, I would like to thank supporters. What do I mean by this? This group includes so many people, such as listeners (subscribers) to my podcast on Apple iTunes who provided five-star reviews. Thank you to everyone who has sent me nice DMs and those who subscribe to my YouTube channel.

Inevitably, there are those who try to tear you down in life. It's rewarding to have had people on the other end of the spectrum providing useful feedback and rooting for me to succeed at everything I've set my mind to accomplishing.

My hope is that I will be one of those people cheering you on some day. Whatever your goals might be—big or small—I would be honored if I played even a minor role in helping you go after them.

I wish all of you much success!

CONTENTS

Introduction *My Dream Is for You to Fulfill Yours, 1*

One *Faith, 7*

Two *The American Way, 21*

Three *The Entrepreneurial Spirit, 35*

Four *Business Relationships, 49*

Five *Hope, 71*

Six *Learning, 87*

Seven *Work Hard, 109*

Eight *The Ability to Create Wealth, 129*

Nine *Stronger Together, 145*

Ten *Taking Action, 157*

Closing Thoughts, *161*

Suggested Reading, 162

About the Author, 167

Darin Batchelder's Podcast, 169

Free 5-Step Process to Passively Investing in Real Estate, 170

INTRODUCTION

My Dream Is for You to Fulfill Yours

You are probably asking four important questions as you flip through the pages in this book . . .

1. *Who am I?*

I'm a business owner, a real estate investor, a Christian, a husband, a father, a friend, a mentor, and a mentee.

2. *What is my background?*

I've succeeded in many aspects of business and life and have learned a great deal over the years from trial and error, successes, and failures. I also admit that I have not fully "arrived" at my final destination and still have a great deal to learn, which makes me uniquely positioned to write this book, as I can relate to people going through a variety of stages of life and business. I continue to learn from others who have come before me and try to become a better person each and every day. I also strongly believe in *building relationships*—with family, friends, partners, investors, vendors, consultants, peers, mentors, mentees, and, of course, the Big Man upstairs. You, the reader of this book, are my next important relationship!

Here are a few more specific things about me: I'm a successful business owner, a real estate investor in over 4,000 multifamily units, a podcast host, and a YouTube content creator. With this book, you can also add author.

1. *Why did I write this book?*

My hope is that this book will provide you with an understanding of how to achieve certain goals as I did and, hopefully, inspire you to chase your own dreams. My biggest joy and reward for writing this book will be when readers tell me that my words have inspired them to take action, enabling them to succeed at a goal and/or make a dream come true.

You *deserve* success, which is why I titled this book *Why* Not *You?* You should not doubt yourself with questions such as *Am I worthy?*, *Am I good enough?*, and *Can I do it?* for even the slightest moment. Maybe you've already experienced some challenges and setbacks. Or maybe you're still struggling to get started, either through lack of motivation or focus. That's okay! Everyone needs a spark. I hope this will be the spark for you. After you've read the book, I encourage you to contact me (see my Author Bio page at the back of the book) and tell me your story. I truly want us to learn and grow together.

2. *Who is this book for?*

This book is geared toward three different types of readers. The first is the individual who is searching for motivation. Perhaps you have an idea, a goal, or a dream you would like to pursue but require some motivation to take action.

Or maybe you are looking for greater focus. This is an easy place for any entrepreneur to get lost. Everything seems exciting when you first start a venture. How does one decide which activities will get you from A to B to C? How does a person stay on track without going after every single shiny object? What does an entrepreneur do when stuck at the starting gate?

I admit, over the years I've had my share of detours and temptations luring me away from my main goals. Controlling your mind and your thoughts—as well as finding work/life balance—is a daily challenge, and I will provide useful tips and advice throughout this book to help you remain on course.

As I see it, the third category of reader is anyone who wants to learn more about me, especially if you are considering investing in real estate projects together. I have good news if you happen to be this type of reader: I'm an open book and confident that you'll have a good sense of who I am in no time.

Now that you know a few things about me and understand my rationale behind writing this book, I'd like to provide a rundown of the contents so you know what to expect and can learn a few insights into my philosophy.

The 10 chapters in this book represent my deeply held beliefs, my opinions. I feel passionate about each and every one: Faith; The American Way; The Entrepreneurial Spirit; Business Relationships; Hope; Learning; Work Hard; The Ability to Create Wealth; Stronger Together, and Taking Action.

I understand that you may not agree with all of my beliefs. Certain things will resonate with you, while others won't. That's completely all right. I'm not here to quiz or judge anyone. Accept the tips, advice, and inspiration you like and feel free to discard the rest.

This book is about your goals, your dreams. My role is to serve, support, and inspire you as best as I can. Let's now begin this journey—together.

ONE

Faith

As a Christian, I decided there was no better place for me to begin this book than with the subject of faith. In this chapter, I will share four of my personal stories of faith in the hope they will help guide you on your first step toward achieving success in life and business.

Two decades ago, my family and I—Tiffany (my wife) and Zack (our 18-month-old son)—lived in Parkland, Florida. At the time, Tiffany was eight months pregnant with our daughter, Kayla. The two of us had already prepared a baby's room, decorating it with a fancy mural of a princess hut on the entire wall.

I don't know why, but every morning when I rose from bed, I would enter the empty baby's room and pray. One such morning, while I was kneeling, the thought entered my mind to pray for my Uncle Javier, who lived in Bolivia. I had just found out that he had cancer. I hadn't seen him in 20-some-odd years—since I was a kid—but internally said a little prayer for him:

God: Please be with Uncle Javier and comfort him and his family. If it's your will, please heal him of his cancer.

I don't know if other people experience this or not but, sometimes when I pray, I hear a gentle whisper. On this occasion, I heard God say the following four words to me: Go visit your uncle.

I couldn't believe what I'd just heard. My mind raced.

Why should I visit him? I haven't seen him in years. What will I do when I get there? Are you sure you want me to go?

An inexplicable, powerful feeling inside coaxed me to head off to Bolivia. It continued throughout the day.

Later on, I told Tiffany about my experience and that I was deliberating on whether I should follow through with the idea. She told me I was crazy.

She was probably right. How could I have even considered it? She was eight months pregnant, and here I was talking about flying to Bolivia to visit my family, who hadn't seen me in years and didn't even know I was coming.

And yet . . . I couldn't shake the feeling. I decided to share what happened during my prayer session with some people in my men's small group. A friend named Scot Sasser, whom I really looked up to from both a Christian and business perspective, said to me, "Look, whenever I felt like God wanted me to do something and I was obedient and did it, good things always happened."

I battled with this decision for several days, during which time I asked my father for my uncle's address. Although he couldn't provide me with one, he did have the name of the hospital where my uncle was being treated.

This piece of information was enough to compel me to make a decision. Somehow, some way, I was going to fly to Bolivia and visit my uncle at the hospital.

I did some research and found I could transfer my frequent flyer miles from one account to another and earn a free trip. Before I knew it, I was on a plane to Bolivia. I didn't have a clue what I was going to do once I landed. I prayed during the flight.

God, why am I going here? Is it to help save my uncle? Am I going there for my cousins? God . . . please just give me the right words.

The plane touched down at around 5:00 a.m. at El Alto Airport, which is about eight miles west of La Paz, Bolivia, where my relatives lived. I didn't know a thing about the country—the culture, the language, or safety precautions—but took a chance and entered a taxi. I doubted the driver spoke any English, so I just gave him the name of the hospital.

He seemed to recognize it and know the way—at least I hoped. We drove for about 15 to 20 minutes through windy, bumpy city roads. It was early and there were few other cars on the streets.

He pulled the taxi along a few cobblestone roads, until we pulled up alongside the side entrance of an old, rundown building. It didn't strike me as a hospital, but I figured it had to be the place, since the driver pointed at the building through the window.

After I paid the driver and exited the vehicle, I was surprised to see that he was following me to the front door. I wondered why, until I noticed gates in front of the doors. The hospital was closed; the doors were locked. The taxi driver stepped in front of me to knock several times.

A nurse approached the door, opening it a crack. I said a few things that drew curious blank stares from her. She didn't know what to make of this English-speaking gringo. My driver intervened, blurting out Spanish words. Her response didn't strike me as receptive. The two exchanged some dialogue; I could tell my driver was attempting to convince her that I was "okay" to allow inside. Whatever he said did the trick. The door opened wider, and I slid through it, making sure my driver heard me say, "Muchas gracias."

"I would like to see my uncle, he's a patient here," I said to her. "His name is Javier Zuazo."

I stepped through the hallway and entered an elevator. Upon reaching our floor, the nurse led me around a bend toward a patient's room. She gestured for me to enter. The room was as plain and no-frills as you could get, which surprised me, since Uncle Javier was a person of means (or so I believed) and owner of Banco Mercantile Santa Cruz S.A., one of the largest banks in La Paz.

As I proceeded forward, I instantly knew I was in the right place. My four cousins, whom I recognized even though I hadn't seen them in a couple of decades, were sleeping on the floor: Darko, Vanessa, Natalia, and Andrea. They had grown up since the last time I'd seen them and, from what I'd heard, were all quite successful—although their sleeping quarters seemed to contradict that. Darko and Vanessa were executives at my uncle's bank.

Darko looked up at me with a groggy eye and sat up in shock. It didn't take long for him to identify me, either.

"Darin? What are you doing here?"

"I don't really know," I grinned. "The idea came to me while I was praying. I felt like God told me to come here and let your dad know that God loves him."

A weak, elderly gentleman stirred on the hospital bed. "Darin? Is that you?"

As I moved closer, I could hardly believe my eyes.

Uncle Javier?

I remembered him as a big, strong, confident, outgoing South American businessman. This patient in the hospital gown lying on the bed was not the same man I once knew.

He grabbed my arm and asked, "Darin, why are you here?"

It didn't bother me that I'd already answered this question to his son. "I don't know, I was praying and felt like God wanted me to come here to tell you that He loves you."

He smiled, visibly humbled that I had undertaken this journey just to see him. His expression made the entire trip worth it.

After my hospital visit, my cousins went out of their way to make sure I had a good time while I was in their country. I stayed in Vanessa's apartment and also visited

Darko's house high up on a hill with a great view overlooking the city. We ate at local restaurants. We talked for hours, catching up and enjoying each other's company. We shared something special that weekend.

My trip home happened way too soon. I was saddened to leave my Bolivian family behind. I prayed during the plane trip . . .

I hope that I did what you wanted me to do. I don't really know what I was there for, but I'm thankful that I went.

When I arrived home, I breathlessly shared my experiences with Tiffany. To my surprise, she seemed equally as excited—but not by my travels.

"Darin, I have to tell you something," she began. "While you were away, it was pretty crazy. I went to church. Afterwards . . . I accepted Christ."

I couldn't believe it. God's underlying plan in sending me to Bolivia had been to save my wife. If He had told me His plan right from the beginning, it's unlikely I would have listened. I probably would have said something like, "There's got to be an easier way."

Sadly, Uncle Javier passed away not long after my visit. I consoled myself with the thought that at least I had made him smile while I was there. I also felt thankful that God had chosen to use me in that fashion to bring my wife closer to Him. As of this writing, Tiffany and I have been married for 23 years. I believe that our individual relationships with God play a major role in our bond with each other.

God works in some crazy, miraculous ways. To this day, I regard this as one of the most impactful stories of my life.

✷ ✷ ✷

One day, while Tiffany and I were parents of young toddlers, she and I had a huge blow-up argument. It reached such a boiling point that I knew I had to leave our house. As I stormed out with my Bible, I deliberated on where I might go to cool off. The one place I knew not to enter was a bar. My father, a recovered alcoholic, had been sober for years. I didn't want to take a chance that running to a bar would become my crutch whenever I had an issue.

I drove for about 20 minutes until a sign for one of those extended-stay hotels caught my eye. I turned into the parking lot, entered the lobby, and asked if they had any available rooms. They did, so I checked in and took the elevator up to my floor with only my keycard, Bible, and a small overnight bag.

I sat on the bed and opened up the Bible, turning to the index. My only thought was to find a way out of my marriage yet still be right with God, so I looked up the word divorce. I flipped back-and-forth to the pages that had a reference to the subject. One after the other, the message was the same: Do not divorce.

"This is not providing me with the out that I was looking for," I grumbled to myself.

I remained in the hotel room for all of 15 minutes. I stood up, left, checked out, and drove straight home. This was the last time I ever considered looking to the Bible for an "out" on anything.

My wife and I made up and, ever since, we have enjoyed the ups and downs of life and marriage while raising two wonderful children. I'm so thankful for God's word, the Bible, which had helped me in that moment to come back and do the work necessary to press on with our marriage.

※ ※ ※

Remember when the dot-com bubble burst back at the turn of the millennium? I happened to work for a tech company right when the pin was about to pop the balloon. It looked like the writing was on the wall that the layoffs were coming.

Tiffany and I struggled over what we were going to do. We were living in a new house with a hefty mortgage that was expensive to maintain, but the last thing we wanted to do was downsize and move. Once again, I looked to my faith for guidance, going to church, praying, and reading the Bible.

Tiffany and I checked out a townhouse for sale. Although it was significantly smaller than where we currently lived, the two of us looked at each other and said, "You know what? We could live here. It's not a big deal. It's just a material place to live. The home is actually wherever we happen to be living; it's us and our family."

I was thankful that we shared the same thought process and that she didn't make me feel like less of a success for being in this financial position. It meant a lot to me.

A week later, as we continued to contemplate the move to the townhouse, a lucrative business opportunity opened up for me and we didn't have to downsize at all. It was as if God had provided for us and taught us a valuable lesson. Material things don't matter in this life; it's all about love, family, relationships, and faith in God.

※ ※ ※

Over the years, I have been part of various men's groups in which members discuss how we can become better men: husbands, fathers, friends, and community members. During the meetings, we typically share tips with each other and provide support and inspiration. I receive a lot of benefit from being part of these groups, and I hope the other men feel the same as I do from my participation.

Flash forward seven or eight years after we changed our minds about downsizing to the townhouse. Our circumstances and mindsets changed, and Tiffany and I decided that we wanted to move from Florida and live closer to her family in Dallas. We also came to the conclusion that the town Prosper, Texas—located about 45 minutes north of Dallas—was a better place to raise our kids, who had turned seven and nine.

We moved into an amazing 5,000-square-foot custom home located at the end of a cul-de-sac with only five other homes on the street. The house was situated on a one-and-a-half-acre plot of land that offered plenty of space for the kids to play. I can't tell you how many Wiffle ball games would end up being played in that backyard!

Once we settled in, I decided not to join a men's group. I admit it: I was just being a bit lazy and probably didn't see the need to meet new people in our church and develop relationships with them.

All of that changed when Moe Harrison, a friend who lived in Frisco—the town next to us—asked me to join his group. "Hey, Darin, there's no pressure. We meet Friday mornings at like 6:00 a.m. If you miss a week here and there, it's not a big deal. It really is no pressure."

The invitation seemed somewhat compelling. Our families had vacationed together while we were in Florida, and they were already living in Texas. Moe had encouraged us about the benefits of Dallas as a place to live and conduct business, which helped us make the decision to move there. We also went to the same church.

I trusted and respected Moe a great deal, but then thought to myself: I often play golf on Thursdays. Do I really want to get up so early for this?

I responded, "Thanks, but no thanks."

Two weeks later, I received an email from Paul Basden, one of the pastors at Preston Trail Community Church in Frisco, asking me to be part of a small group. There was a catch.

"Look," he wrote, "we're going to have accountability.

First of all, we want to have each of the guys meet on a Saturday from 9:00 in the morning to 3:00 in the afternoon and get to know one another. Secondly, we expect you to read whatever the lesson is and participate and commit to being in the group for a year."

This posed quite an internal challenge for me. I'd already said "No" to the first request from my friend; how could I possibly turn down the pastor?

It dawned on me that this was God's way of saying to me:

Hey, Darin—man, you said no to the other one. Here's the pastor inviting you. You can't say no again.

So, I joined this men's group and abided by the rules. And I'm so glad I did. As of this writing, I've been part of it for four years. I've developed authentic relationships with these men and am so thankful that we learn about God while sharing our daily struggles and providing encouragement and guidance to each other.

✺ ✺ ✺

I hope you enjoyed these four stories and took something away from each of them. I believe we all need to have faith in our private lives and in business. Our loved ones, friends, community members, and neighbors all play important roles in our success, as do business partners, direct reports, customers, vendors, and many other professionals. To accomplish anything, you must have a strong team supporting you.

I believe the biggest team member of all is the Big Man upstairs. With God on your side, all things are possible.

TWO

The American Way

America: land of the free, home of the brave.

This saying may seem like a cliché, but I believe in it. I love our country. The United States of America is powerful—its history, its economy, its resolve, and its determination.

I'm a glass half-full kind of guy when it comes to where our nation is headed. I know, we are divided politically and there are many issues that have caused great division among American citizens. Despite all this and our recent turmoil, I still believe there is no place in the world that offers such a wealth of opportunity. I remain optimistic that we will pull through stronger than ever, as we always do.

I support what has become known as "The American Way." But what does this really mean? Is it the cliché of "life, liberty, and happiness"? Is it the American Dream of owning your home? Financial freedom? A life of luxury? In this chapter, I will explain my philosophy on the subject without getting into any politics.

In my mind, The American Way is the promise that all citizens have the opportunity to chase and fulfill their goals and dreams. Our country has had a remarkable history of iconic entrepreneurs—from past pioneers such as Henry Ford, Andrew Carnegie, and John D. Rockefeller to present-day icons Bill Gates, Jeff Bezos, and Elon Musk. Whether you personally like these individuals or not doesn't matter; they symbolize free enterprise, business savvy, and the achievement of the American Dream.

THE LAND OF OPPORTUNITY

If you want to achieve your dream badly enough, America offers unlimited opportunities to help you find a way to grow, accomplish your goals, and fulfill your dreams. Our country was built on the entrepreneurial aspirations and dreams of people who set their sights high and established everything from long-running small family companies to business empires. This includes Americans who were born here, as well as immigrants who arrived on our shores without any money, educated themselves, and then went out on their own to become business owners.

Opportunity is often defined as "a set of circumstances that make it *possible* to do something." Note that I stressed the word possible. If you do nothing and don't take action, you will miss opportunities.

I have personally interviewed many successful people in my field—the multifamily real estate investing arena—and they worked hard to find ways to excel and achieve—often against incredible odds. (Later in this chapter, I will introduce you to two such remarkable individuals.) Often their first attempts didn't work, and they had to pivot and try something else. But they had great determination and belief in themselves, which enabled them to press on. These entrepreneurs have achieved, if not exceeded, their goals. That's because they continued to set increasingly bigger goals.

TRAPPED IN THEIR OWN FEAR

Along with the success stories, I've met plenty of people who believe they're trapped in whatever job they happen to be doing and can't even think about trying something else. I couldn't disagree more. For one thing, fear of failure paralyzes a lot of people. I understand that risk-taking and heading off into the unknown with starting a business can seem scary to them. Why? Because they have jobs that earn them paychecks and they are terrified they will not be able to make the same amount of money if they were to go off on their own. They have become slaves to the house, the cars, the credit card debt, and so on, which are paid for by the hard-earned income they have been earning from their jobs.

What guarantee does a person have of earning the same or higher salary if he or she were to start a business? None. Certainly, one shouldn't expect the riches to come right out of the starting gate. It takes a while to put the business together, figure out what works and what doesn't, and begin to get into a groove and find momentum.

People have asked me: "Darin, what was the hardest part of starting your business?"

I answer them by saying, "Signing the lease to the office space."

They give me a funny look and ask, "I don't get it. Why was that the hardest part? Was it a long-term lease? Was it expensive?"

"No," I reply. "Signing the lease made it real. It meant that I had to tell my family, my old colleagues, my friends, and my old customers that I was in business for real. There was no turning back. How would I explain to people if I fail?"

And yet, with all the highs and lows I've faced, I have never turned back. American perseverance means you muster the courage to stay the course and plow through, even during the most difficult times.

AMERICANS LOVE TO SPEND

One of the things holding people back from going after their American Dream is that they spend money as soon as they earn it. It burns holes right through their pockets. An employee who earns a well-deserved bonus or raise spends the money before the deposit has even cleared. Without money in the bank—and especially if you have a lot of credit card debt—it becomes difficult to sock away money to invest in starting a business and/or have pocket money in case the financial situation goes south.

While it's a wonderful thing that Americans have the privilege of living a high quality of life, it's equally as dangerous that succumbing to the temptation to buy is as easy as a few keystrokes on a keyboard or phone. We tend to buy stuff rather than go after our long-term goals. I believe that the fancy car, bigger house, extravagant boat, etc., mentally hurt people. The purchases give immediate pleasure but extinguish the fire in the belly to follow a lifelong dream. I believe that life is too short to waste away making other people money.

That's not to say you can't enjoy life and reward yourself every now and then. Just make sure you stay focused on your medium-to-long-term goals, which typically require you to make sacrifices in the present to benefit you in the future.

DO YOU NEED TO CONCEIVE THE GREAT AMERICAN IDEA?

The other thing that I've found going to conferences—more so entrepreneurial ones than real estate—is that the modern-day person thinks he or she needs to create the one spectacular idea that has never been done before. The individual doesn't believe success is at all possible if the idea doesn't surface right away with the stars completely aligned. He or she also becomes convinced that lots of money needs to miraculously appear to subsidize the idea for it to fly. When this magical combination doesn't descend from thin air, these folks tell themselves it was never meant to be and give up without even trying.

Here's my little secret: You don't need that unique business idea at all! In fact, most flourishing businesses begin from a previously existing business concept. Either they add a twist to it, do it better, make it more affordable, or transform it into an upscale product or service. It could be as simple as something like offering better customer service than the competition.

Consider the YETI company, which produces outdoor travel accessories like coolers, mugs, and duffel bags. How long have we had coolers? How long has it been since the invention of the coffee mug? YETI didn't originate either of these concepts and yet they created a company worth $1.5 billion dollars. What did this all-American company do that was embraced by so many people? They designed better products. The coolers keep the liquid colder, while the mugs sustain heat longer. Then they created a brand around it that everybody wanted to be a part of and—bam! Breakthrough success.

Let's talk about Uber. They are currently the best-known transportation service in America, and they are growing exponentially around the world. Did Uber invent the taxi? No, of course not; actually, they reinvented it by blending technology (an app) that connects riders with available drivers in their vicinity. As if that's not enough, they added the element of entrepreneurialism for the drivers, who could function independently in their own safe vehicles while building their own reputations. In this way, Uber has transformed the way people travel from one place to another and stepped up the game in the car service industry.

The American Way may or may not involve being the actual originator of the basic idea. But it does require creativity, scrappiness, fearlessness, tenacity, determination, persistence, and the ability to bootstrap when needed.

TWO REAL-LIFE STORIES OF THE AMERICAN DREAM

I would like to share two successful multifamily real estate investor stories: David Lagat and Ramana Korada. I recently had the privilege of interviewing these investors on my podcast. As it happens, these two gentlemen came to the United States to attend college. They arrived with little money and didn't have any support in this country, as they were the first family members to arrive here. I was not surprised to hear both gentlemen refer to America as "the land of opportunity."

David's Story: *From Cow Monopoly to Wheeling and Dealing Apartment Complexes*

David Lagat was born and raised in Kenya. In that country, the real-life game of Monopoly—i.e., the process of building wealth—is determined by who has the greatest number of cows. (Yes, that is for real.) Growing up, David believed he would someday build wealth as a cow owner.

Things changed quite a bit when he arrived in the United States to major in finance at Texas Christian University (TCU). He studied, graduated, and landed a job in the banking industry. Then an interesting thing happened. David—who was about to do what many people in the United States do, buy his first house—ran into an older gentleman who changed the course of his life. This man advised him, "Don't buy a house—instead, purchase a duplex, fourplex, or whatever you can afford. Live in one unit and rent out the rest."

David took his advice and bought his first investment property. He took the equity built up from the first and purchased another one . . . then another . . . and then another. Today, with his company, Bella Asset Management, he is an owner in thousands of multifamily units.

Here's my view of what David did right. First, he came to the United States with the positive mindset that it is the land of opportunity. He did not complain or blame others for his struggles to become educated, get a job, and start a business. Instead, he followed the advice of someone older and wiser. Then he took action. There was some sacrifice and risk early on, but he had faith that he would benefit later on—which he ultimately did.

Ramana's Story: *From Small Town to Big-Time Multifamily Real Estate Investor*

Like David, Ramana Korada was the first in his family to immigrate to the United States. He grew up in a small town in India of about 2,000 people, approximately 300 of whom were part of his family.

He came to America with little money to attend the University of Texas at El Paso, where he studied electrical/computer engineering. On graduation, he became an IT consultant. His learning didn't stop there, though. He saved his money and searched for ways to invest his money. His first investment in a tech startup didn't pan out as he would have liked, so he shifted to real estate, investing in a couple of retail strip centers. Unable to secure retail deals that excited other investors, he entered a multifamily investing mentorship group. Eventually, he partnered with Venkat Avasarala, another member of the group, and formed Raven Multifamily. Together, they have since closed a dozen syndications, raising $80 million to invest in these multifamily deals.

What did Ramana do right? Like David, he arrived in America believing it was the land of opportunity and started with a positive mindset. Next, he saved money to put into investments. His first attempts may not have worked out, but that didn't stop him. He persisted, continuing to search for the right breakthrough opportunity. He had faith in himself and that his continued efforts would lead to success. With Raven Multifamily, he has accomplished all of this and more, investing in 3,000 multifamily units.

Americans: Go for It

When people approach me and ask for advice on whether they should start a business, I always encourage them to go for it and take a chance. There has never been a single occasion when one of those individuals has later come back to me and said, "Darin, you know what? That was bad advice you gave me. I wish I'd never started my business—it was a mistake."

This says a lot but, of course, it doesn't mean that every single person was successful right out of the gate. There were plenty of times when they ran with their idea and, for whatever reason, it just didn't work. As a testament to their American spirit, however, they didn't give up. Instead, they pivoted to something else. Their initial idea didn't work—so what? They simply went on to something else and found a new path that eventually did work out.

Napoleon Hill, author of *Think and Grow Rich*, once said, "Whatever your mind can conceive and believe, it can achieve."

Think back to the California Gold Rush, which began in 1848 and flourished a year later. Families impulsively packed up their things and traveled across dangerous terrain on horse-drawn carriages to reach the Sacramento Valley. Why did they take such a high risk? They sought a better life for themselves and their families. They were willing to do whatever it took to obtain the American Dream.

If you are someone who is happy working for someone else—whether a small business or a big corporation—that is perfectly fine by me. Your American Dream may involve getting a good paycheck and owning your own home. There is nothing wrong with that. If this happens to be the case, I'm not writing to you. I'm addressing those among you who hunger to go out on your own.

You long to start a company or make a living off your investments. You want financial freedom and the ability to control your own destiny.

Imagine. *You can be your own boss. You can support your family by creating something remarkable and sustainable. You can serve others through your creation.*

My advice: Stop making excuses! Don't blame the government, your upbringing, bad luck, your family, your boss, your finances, or your specific situation. We've all had our share of challenges, some of us more than others. No matter what obstacles and dilemmas you may be facing, keep in mind there is always someone—one of your fellow American citizens—who has had it much worse, and yet managed to find a way to accomplish his or her goals.

Don't delay! Avoid procrastinating! Put this book down and get started on the path to fulfilling your American Dream. Make the decision that you are going to take a chance. At the end of the day, you will never be happy unless you try. You don't want to live your entire life and then have regrets later on. Don't let life turn you into another nine to five worker who hates his or her job and feels trapped.

If you believe you can achieve your dream, you will find a way. Surround yourself with people who will encourage you. Learn from others who have been down a similar path in your field or industry.

America is still the land of opportunity. Go out and grab it for yourself!

And now that we have established the importance of The American Way, we are ready to move on to focusing 100 percent on "The Entrepreneurial Spirit" in Chapter Three.

THREE

The Entrepreneurial Spirit

How do you know if you have *the entrepreneurial spirit*? *Think. Listen to your gut.*

Do you feel like you have a pit in your stomach about an idea you've always wanted to accomplish? Have you let life circumstances or fear stop you from even trying?

I believe that God made each and every one of us unique. We all have special talents to help serve others. When we are empowered with that purpose, we are capable of accomplishing *anything*.

WHAT IS AN ENTREPRENEUR?

An entrepreneur is simply someone who has an idea for a product or service and makes the decision to execute on his or her vision. There are many characteristics of entrepreneurs, such as the ability to:

- Create a vision
- Execute on the vision
- Make quick decisions without 100 percent information
- Be action-oriented
- Have confidence in themselves
- Inspire other people to help execute on the vision
- Avoid worrying about what other people might say or think
- Seek counsel from people who have already done what they are about to do
- Be determined
- Be persistent
- Be a self-starter
- Have passion
- Be eager to learn

That's a long list! You don't need to master every one of these skills at first. To start, it's most important to create a vision and to follow through on it, no matter what it takes. Other skills can be learned along the way.

Don't allow checking off every box to stop you from getting started!

Wealthy entrepreneurs do not make excuses—*they just do the work*. These are some of the excuses I hear all the time:

"I'm too old . . ."
"People tell me it won't work . . ."
"I know others who tried, failed . . ."
"I don't have good luck . . ."
"I'm not smart enough . . ."
"I'm not good enough . . ."
"I don't have enough money to get started . . ."
"I have a family to support . . ."

If you find yourself hearing, thinking, or saying any of these things, drown them out and move forward anyway. *There is no excuse*! There are billionaires out there who aren't half as smart as you are. There are plenty of wealthy entrepreneurs who started out with little or no money and had families to support. That didn't stop them from doing what was needed to feed their families and pay the bills, but they squirreled away time and worked twice as hard to meet their goals. If they can do it, so can you!

The Entrepreneurial Spirit

TECHNIQUES FROM MASTER ENTREPRENEURS

I've had a number of remarkable people on my podcast. Many of them were self-made successes and overcame great obstacles to become successes. While there are some distinctions in their approaches, there are also some interesting similarities. In the following three sections, you'll learn from three of the best: Swapnil Agarwal, Vinney (Smile) Chopra, and Kim Radaker Bays.

Swapnil Agarwal: *Failure Is Not an Option*

Raised in a small town in India, Swapnil Agarwal came to the United States with his parents when he was 15 years old. He attended high school in the Houston area and graduated from the University of Texas in Austin. He began his career working for a private equity firm in Hong Kong, where he lived for about eight years. On his return to America, he founded Nitya Capital (current annual net revenue: $171 million) and Karya Property Management (current annual revenue: $156 million). In 2017, he was honored with the Ernst & Young Entrepreneur of the Year Award.

As of this writing, Swapnil is only 40 years old. It's clear he has independently made it to the top in real estate, investment banking, and private equity. But how did he do it? What makes him different? What makes him special?

First, he made a decision to start his own company. Next, he committed himself to making this happen. It's that simple. These are the two steps every entrepreneur needs to do: (1) decide and (2) commit.

That's not to say Swapnil met with overnight success with Nitya Capital. The private equity real estate firm had humble beginnings, starting with one investment property. He found the opportunity on Loopnet—an online marketplace for property—and it was a fully marketed deal. As virtually anyone in the multifamily investment business will tell you, deals offered on Loopnet are typically those that have been passed on by most other investors. His risk paid off. In 2013, this 37-unit multifamily property was valued at $1 million. Flash forward to today: Nitya Capital manages over $2 billion in total assets consisting of 20,000 multifamily units.

How did he meet with such astronomical growth over an eight-year stretch? His answer (and mine, too): *mindset*!

Swapnil believed he could do it. He does not accept failure as an option. Sure, he knows there will be bumps along the road. Things don't always work out as intended. Challenges pop up left and right. But Swapnil pivots; he does not give up and quit. Instead, he keeps learning, adapting, and making decisions with the best information available.

I often like to ask guests on my podcast if they have a next big stretch goal and, if so, might they share it with my listeners. I was especially curious about what Swapnil would have to say in response. Here's a guy who reached $2 billion in assets by 40. What could possibly be bigger than that?

"*One hundred billion* in assets under management," he answered.

Awesome. Incredible. Talk about a stretch goal! That is the perfect example of entrepreneurial mindset at its best. I have no doubt that he truly believes he will achieve it. He has, therefore, followed the two easy steps I mentioned earlier: (1) decide and (2) commit.

I look forward to watching him make that goal happen. Along the way, he will continue to inspire many others to go after their goals and dreams.

That's another special byproduct of being an entrepreneur: Others just starting out on their own journeys look to others for inspiration to make their dreams happen.

Vinney (Smile) Chopra: *His Glass Is Half-Full*

Vinney (Smile) Chopra (aka "Mr. Smiles") also comes from India and has a remarkable rags-to-riches story.

Vinney arrived in the United States four decades ago with only $7 in his pocket. Over the years, he's completed over 30 multifamily syndications while his company, Moneil Investment Group, manages $300 million in assets with over 4,000 units.

It goes without saying success was not handed to Vinney. He believed in himself. He worked hard. He learned from experts. He focused his positive energy on helping others. It's no wonder he's earned the nickname "Mr. Smiles," which is evident just by hearing the demeanor in his voice. He has always believed in individuals' ability to shape the world around them through positive thought and selfless actions.

Now 70 years old, Vinney lives in the San Francisco Bay area. He's an accomplished speaker with 10,000 speeches to date and the bestselling author of Apartment Syndication Made Easy and Positivity Brings Profitability.

How has Vinney achieved such mind boggling self-made success? You guessed it— positive mindset. It would be a major understatement to say he's a glass half-full kind of guy. Vinney plans to continue to live a full life and never stop helping others. I'm confident he will make that happen.

Kim Radaker Bays: *Pushing the Envelope*

Kim Radaker Bays is an example of an entrepreneur who keeps pushing the boundaries. She challenges her team (and herself) with questions like the following:

- How can we be more efficient?
- How can we bring more value?
- How can we do things better?
- How can we impact more people?

Kim has been in the multifamily investing space for about a decade. For her, it wasn't enough to learn how to syndicate and purchase large, multifamily properties. She took it to another level, working to create vertical integration. What does that mean? It basically refers to ways she could create more value for investors and tenants by establishing new complementary companies. She formed Exponential Property to purchase value-add multifamily properties. She then decided to bring property management in house, so they could better control the day-to-day operations. She took another major step forward by founding Exist Multifamily, which purchases materials for the interior rehab of units from overseas in full containers, resulting in significant savings on materials. She identified efficiencies by boxing up the materials separately and then delivering them straight in those boxes to each of the properties.

This is a powerful idea. Why? Each multifamily unit that is rehabbed is different. Some need the majority of materials changed out, while others only require a few to be replaced. This is important because it prevents the rehab personnel from having to go back-and-forth to a storage unit at the property to get the materials. It also improves inventory management and limits inventory loss. This may sound like a minor issue, but when you consider being involved in 22 multifamily properties consisting of over 7,000 units, efficiencies and safeguards concerning inventory can play a substantial role in maximizing returns to investors.

Kim didn't stop there. She brought the internal rehab in house as well. She's also searching for ways to become more efficient, productive, and profitable. Her latest step was to internally start yet another company, Exist Graphics, which creates branding and designs for signage, embroidery for workers' uniforms, swag, etc.

The Entrepreneurial Spirit 43

Kim's thoughts and focus are always on other people. In addition to the questions mentioned earlier, she is constantly seeking to help:

- Maximize investor returns
- Grow the wealth of others
- Best serve her employees
- Provide a better community for tenants

I've heard this expression repeated many times over: If you want to be wealthy, help others become wealthy. Kim embodies this sentiment to the fullest. When I asked for her stretch goal she answered, "Help create one hundred millionaires by investing in our multifamily deals."

There you have it. Successful entrepreneurs help others!

**GETTING STARTED: OVERCOMING FEAR—
THE ENTREPRENEURIAL CURSE**

How do you fulfill your entrepreneurial goals? Most likely, it's by taking that idea lodged in the pit of your stomach and taking action to make it happen. Some of you might be skeptical and say, "Darin, that's easy for you to say.

You've found a niche and built your business. My entrepreneurial dream is different."

How do I respond to that? By stating the following: "The only difference between you and me is that I took a chance and chased the idea that had caused the pit in my stomach to form in the first place. Once I achieved success, a new idea popped up that I also deliberately went after."

I started my own company trading loan portfolios back in 2007. A decade later, I invested in my first real estate deal—a duplex—which led to my joining a multifamily mentorship group. A year later, in 2018, I began to invest passively into other syndicators' deals. Twelve months later, I was a general partner and lead syndicator in a 76-unit townhome community in the Dallas–Fort Worth area. A couple of years after that, I launched my podcast. In 2021, my YouTube channel went live. That same year, I started writing this book.

Look, each one of those steps was scary. At first, I didn't have a clue how I was going to accomplish any of those things. But I went after them. I made decisions and pursued my goals. I sought out people who had done them before and learned from them. Deep down, I know that fear is the main thing that holds people back—even though they don't admit it.

You need to recognize that everyone experiences such fears. Have you ever seen an interview with a famous singer, musician, actor, or comedian when he or she is asked, "Are you still scared to go on stage or in front of a camera?" From the interviews I've seen, the answer goes something like this: "Of course I'm scared and nervous. But once I'm up there, I love it!"

For example, singer Adele once admitted in Rolling Stone: "I'm scared of audiences." She must pull together a lot of courage to get out there, even with all of her talent and success with adoring crowds.

Similarly, opera singer Andrea Bocelli fears he will not meet audience expectations. He finds a way to push past it and get himself out on stage. Once there, he settles in and performs magnificently.

We are all human. Fear and the limiting beliefs in our heads will stop us from reaching our potential, if we allow this to happen. I've had thoughts like: What if nobody listens to my podcast? What if nobody reads this book? What if no one clicks Like on my social media posts? These were all negative thoughts driven by fear, but I didn't allow them to hold me back from taking a chance and acting on achieving my goals. One of the sayings I like to tell people is that they need to "Push past their fear."

Over the years, I've always spoken to my kids before they headed off to their first day of school. "When you sit down in class," I say, "smile and say 'hello' to the student next to you." Why do I coach them on doing such a basic thing? Because not only am I well aware that my kids are nervous, I also recognize that all kids are scared on day one. I knew that if they were to follow my advice, my kids would become more confident, and the other students will feel better.

Entrepreneurs—like kids on their first day of school—are terrified of taking that first step. Don't let anyone tell you otherwise. Even Mark Cuban—the extremely confident billionaire entrepreneur and Shark on the TV show Shark Tank—has gone on record saying he was scared when he started out.

My advice to you when you are bringing your idea out into the world is similar to what I tell my kids: Smile, say hello, and go for it! You have nothing to lose. Sure, there will always be doubters and people who judge you. There may even be a couple who have their own self-esteem issues and are so jealous that they hope you fail. That's their problem, not yours! You are not taking a chance for them. You are throwing yourself out there to pursue your goals and, in doing so, to help others.

In my world—the multifamily real estate investing space—I'm rewarded by helping people grow their wealth. I feel a sense of accomplishment and pride by helping others achieve their financial goals. I'm also rewarded by seeing the improvement in multifamily communities when we spend rehab dollars to repair and/or improve the property. When the work has been completed, it's an amazing feeling to hear a long-term tenant offer his "Thanks!" while praising all the noticeable improvements.

Why do I share all of this with you? I want to inspire you and others to take a chance and give back to society. Trust that you have unique ideas that, once executed, will be monetized and contribute to the lives of other people.

So, do I stop there? Not a chance. Right when I seek to achieve a goal, initiate a fresh idea, or overcome a new challenge, I react to that sensation—the pit in my stomach—and march forward to get it done.

To me, this is what the entrepreneurial spirit is all about: pushing past the fear; continuing on when you hit roadblocks and setbacks; and being persistent until you are even closer to fulfilling your dream. And then . . . you move on to your next goal!

FOUR

Business Relationships

As we begin, I'd like to clarify that this chapter is not going to be about relationships in terms of friends and family. Instead, I'm going to focus on three different kinds of business relationships:

- Investors
- Business partners
- Mentors

Before we get into the subject of business relationships, I want to emphasize that family and friends are extremely important to me. They are a higher priority in my life before any business or monetary goals. Frankly, I don't know how I would ever have gotten by without them.

I hope that you will take a step back and look at the most important people in your life and think about what they mean to you. Once you begin to truly see and understand their emotional value to you and how they influenced the person you have become, you will appreciate them all the more—and perhaps become an even better father/mother, sister/brother, husband/wife, and son/daughter.

There is probably no role in life more challenging than those of husband/wife and father/mother. It is not possible for anyone to be "perfect." Speaking for myself, I admit that I have done well in these areas at times and have failed at others.

I am a firm believer in self-development. There will always be people ahead of you to learn from and people behind you who can learn from you. This giving and receiving of knowledge is a huge blessing and is what life is all about.

INVESTING IN BUSINESS—AND IN YOURSELF

If you are starting out as an entrepreneur and/or small business owner, the idea of getting an *investor* may seem to carry so much weight it feels intimidating and out of reach. I hear these negative statements and questions all the time:

- "I'm too afraid to ask for money."
- "I don't know how to do a business plan."
- "What if they turn me down and don't invest in my business?"
- "I don't want to be responsible for losing other people's money."
- "What if I can't get enough investors aboard to close my deal?"
- "How do I know if I can trust the investors?"
- "I worry that I don't understand the fine print and may be getting ripped off."
- "I don't want to give away control of my company."
- "What if I decide I don't like the investors—how do I get out of it?"

There is no reason to have any hesitation when it comes to bringing in outside people to help jumpstart your business idea. Investors are there to make a simple decision: *If I put money into your business, will I earn enough to turn a profit in the short- and/or long-term?* Most investors are hungry and crave new things to invest in that fit their strategies. Some of them even have *too much* excess cash and need to find opportunities to roll it into right away. Since investors are putting their money on the line, they *want* your business to be a success; it would be extremely rare for them to do it purely out of goodwill or as a write-off. Chances are, many of them probably stood in your shoes early on in their careers, looking for ways to raise capital to subsidize their businesses.

All of this means that they aren't considering investing in your business just to criticize and find fault—or to take advantage (although, of course, they'll want a good deal). They are in the process of:

1. Analyzing your business financials
2. Looking for growth
3. Probing the leadership team for talent, innovation, and excellence
4. Determining the company's unique selling proposition (USP)
5. Assessing the market size and trends
6. Figuring out if your business model is sustainable

Outside the aforementioned half-dozen main issues, investors need to know if they can trust you as much as you need to trust them. When asked about potential risks, you must be as transparent as possible. It's also ideal to know your company's numbers, show your passion, demonstrate your commitment to the business, and convey that you have something irresistible other businesses can't offer.

At the same time, your intent is to help them feel secure investing with you. You must build trust and educate them on how investing will benefit them. If they can check off the boxes of the half-dozen previously cited items regarding your business, value the company right, provide the necessary capital, and trust you and your team, they will be more than happy to invest in your business.

The problem with most entrepreneurial thinking is that it tends to be too focused on the person putting the deal together—i.e., *me* focused. Instead, try the reverse: Start thinking about *what's in it for other people*, namely the investors. A lot of this has to do with establishing the right mindset. Are you trying to get other people's money so you can close your deal—or are you presenting an opportunity that has the potential to grow the wealth of the investor?

Investor relationships can take a while to develop. Although investors may trust you enough to make the deal, *complete* trust must be earned and built over time with transparency, good communication, and measurable results (i.e., profit).

BECOMING AN INVESTOR

Now it's time to turn the tables and let you in on a little secret: The same fears experienced by business owners are shared by investors. They are often scared of taking the plunge, too! Their capital is on the line, and they don't want to make a mistake that will cost them. Similarly, they don't want to miss out on a potential golden opportunity. Every investor has a different business strategy and risk tolerance level. Before jumping into the fray, give some serious thought to your business strategy and how much risk you are willing to take. But once you take the leap, stay the course!

I'd like to share a story from when I was first getting started. I had already passively invested in a number of deals, and I knew I wanted to become a syndicator/general partner. Many people suggested an interim step of becoming a key principal (KP) in a deal. I asked three questions:

1. What is involved?
2. What is the benefit?
3. How do I go about becoming one?

I learned that being a KP means you are a part of the sponsorship team on the deal. Your balance sheet and liquidity will be combined with others on the team to qualify for the loan, which you are required to sign. In some instances, a KP will be compensated by obtaining a percentage of the GP ownership for performing this duty; in my case, however, there was no extra compensation.

My wife asked me, "So, why are you trying so hard to become a KP? It sounds like we're taking on more risk without being compensated for it."

I laughed in agreement and then said, "Here's the thing. If I become a KP, then I'm in the database for Fannie Mae or Freddie Mac, and it makes it easier to get future loans with the agencies by having that experience."

It was a risk, but one I was willing to take. I knew, liked, and trusted the sponsors of the deal, and I decided to move forward as a KP.

That was back in 2018 when my wife and I invested $100,000. Flash forward to the present; we sold that property and received our $100,000 principal back—plus *another* $100,000+. Wow, we doubled our investment! That is a fantastic return over three years.

Could this deal have gone south? Absolutely. But we believed in the opportunity. We invested with good people. If the deal had struggled, we knew the sponsors would have done everything in their power to right the ship. There are never any guarantees when you are an investor. In a mutually beneficial investor relationship, the business does its best to maximize returns while we support them in their efforts.

I continue to invest as a limited partner, a KP, and as a general partner (GP). I'm thankful for the investors who invest alongside me, and I wholeheartedly believe that the deals we invest in will help grow wealth for everyone concerned. I also appreciate the sponsors that I invest with passively.

Keep this in mind: There are always going to be investors out there looking for deals to help them make their dreams come true. The sooner you realize it's about *their* goals and dreams and not yours, the greater the likelihood you will be able to create a solid, profitable relationship and then model it for future deals.

PARTNERING UP

In the world of large-scale multifamily—60-plus units and up—it's nearly impossible to land your first syndication deal without partnering with someone who is experienced and successful. Brokers, lenders, and investors will not take you seriously unless an accomplished partner is involved in the deal.

These are some of the excuses I hear from people about getting involved in partnerships:

- "Why would anyone want to partner with me?"
- "I'm too young."
- "I'm too old."
- "I don't have enough experience."
- "I don't have enough money."
- "I don't know how to raise money."

The list goes on. Here's my response to all of them: There is no excuse! If you want to get in the game, start out by identifying a suitable business partner.

Why do people partner in the first place? Because each person brings value to the table. They are better together than individually.

"Ok, Darin," you say. "What does that mean for my situation?"

Large-scale multifamily deals are basically about three things: *finding deals; attracting investors; and asset management.* Think about where you can add value in the process by answering these questions:

- Do you have lots of capital to invest?
- Do you have a strong network of people who can bring capital to these deals?
- Are you driven to achieve success?
- Do you have time to focus on finding deals?

If you answered *yes* to any of the above questions, it means you are more than capable of adding value in terms of finding deals and attracting investors. Once your mind accepts that you have value to offer, the next step is to find someone who supplements your experience. If you are young, driven, persistent, and willing to do the work, your action plan would be to search for a partner who has the experience and deal-making reputation that you lack, plus a strong balance sheet and investor base.

You are probably asking, "Okay, how do I find such a partner?"

Good question. Below are just a few ideas:

- Join a multifamily mentorship group.
- Attend free multifamily meetup groups.
- Join online multifamily Facebook groups and then send private messages to connect with people.
- Listen to podcasts and read books by experts on the subject and then approach them.
- Ask your network if they can refer anyone in their communities.

You also might want to find out what types of deals the experienced syndicator is looking for and see what would be valuable to him or her. It could be possible to find deals that fit the syndicator's parameters. Another option may be to find an opportunity that the syndicator wasn't even looking at but may have interest in. For example, he or she may be looking for properties with 200+ units, while you are focusing on 100–200 units. If you bring such a property to his attention, you are adding significant value to him.

Be creative—you could try searching in another geographic area or for smaller deals or older vintage opportunities. The syndicator may not be hunting for those unusual deals, which means there might be an open niche for you.

In my case, it took a while for me to figure this out. Originally, I began by trying to talk to experienced syndicators while playing the "nice guy" card. "Hey, I'm a good guy—do you want to partner with me?" I offered to do free work, underwrite, come along on property visits, and do whatever would help. Many syndicators were cordial and answered, "Sure Darin, if the right opportunity comes up" or "I'll let you know."

Nobody did.

One evening, over beers, a syndicator shared some friendly advice with me. "Darin, you know what, if I get a deal under contract, do you think I'm going to ask you to be my partner? No, I'm going to ask that guy over there. Why? Because he has proven experience and already has relationships with brokers, lenders, and investors."

"Oh, I get it," I realized. "Then why would you or anyone ever partner with a new guy like me?"

"Go find me the deal!" she responded.

That was my eye-opening moment. From that point forward, I followed her advice and sought out deals where fewer people were looking. I underwrote all the deals I could find in the Dallas–Fort Worth area, focusing on opportunities between 60 and 100 units. As I previously mentioned, experienced syndicators were typically chasing deals of 100-plus units, so I figured this was my chance to knock out some of the competition. If I had a deal where the numbers looked like they might work, I then obtained a budget from a property management company. I also obtained loan quotes. I went on a tour of the property. I visited other multifamily properties in the area to assess the competition and determine how much I thought we could raise rents, if we were to invest rehab money into the property. I developed a relationship with the broker to get a better feel for where this deal might trade.

Once all these details came together on the deal, that's when I made the phone call to an experienced syndicator to see if he had any interest in pursuing it. I laid everything out for him. Since he was familiar with the area and everything seemed in order, he agreed to partner with me. I had done all the work up to that point, so he had nothing to lose. I knew I couldn't close the deal without the experience and support of a veteran multifamily investor, so it was a win-win situation for both of us.

I gained experience, knowledge, contacts, and confidence with every deal I initiated. It reached a point where I had five or more solid, experienced syndicators who trusted me enough to consider partnering with me if I came across the right opportunities.

If you are just starting out, I highly recommend having three, four, or even five experienced syndicators you can take a deal to. You don't want to do all that work and make an excited phone call, just to find out the guy you'd pegged for it is too busy working on another deal to partner with you. If you can't come up with someone quickly, you risk losing credibility with the broker, lenders, and investors you discussed the deal with.

Don't worry: You've got this! There are partners out there who are just waiting for someone like you for a partner relationship. All you need to do is go out there and track them down.

MENTORING ISN'T JUST FOR KIDS

You may have a picture in your head of what a mentor is: a big brother or sister to a child or teenager who helps share life skills and provide advice. But what is the actual definition of a mentor?

The word mentor means: *an experienced and trusted advisor*.

For adults in the workforce, there are many different

types of mentors—paid and unpaid. People have different views on the value of working with one. If you haven't guessed this already, I'm an advocate of the mentoring concept.

I also believe that, if you truly want to achieve something, find someone who has already done it and learn from that person. There is massive value in learning from others who have "been there and done that." For starters, you can avoid obvious pitfalls and mistakes.

You are probably thinking: *Why should I bother? There is a ton of free information out there. Why waste my time with a mentor? I can just Google or YouTube just about anything these days.*

Here's the problem: How much time will you spend scrolling through these sites trying to find the *right* information? Then it's usually piecemeal. Maybe you'll find a tiny bit of valuable information here or there, but then you need to organize and prioritize it. Not only that, you can't always rely on these sites to be reliable and accurate; some of them may even offer conflicting information, which will only confuse you.

In my case, I always seek out the best-in-class mentors and consultants and hire them to teach me how to accomplish my goals in the most efficient, lucrative way.

I may end up spending more to hire the best, but I think it's completely worth it.

Below are some examples of places where I discovered mentoring expertise:

- **Conferences:** I attend many paid conferences in the real estate investing, leadership, and entrepreneurial spaces. When I'm an attendee listening to several speakers in a day, I'm listening for things I can act on and apply to my life and business right away. Sometimes the events go on and on without providing value and then, all of a sudden, the fourth speaker says something that is relevant and directly applicable to me. I think to myself: *Wow! If I apply that to my business, it can be huge! That one nugget was well worth sitting through these other speakers and, for sure, the ticket price.*

- **Social Media:** Many entrepreneurs told me they gained a lot of business by building up their social media networks. This struck me as funny because I thought Instagram was just a little picture app my teenagers used. I didn't have an Instagram account and didn't understand it one bit. I told my wife,

"I'm attending this conference—and I'm going to find someone who knows Instagram and hire him to help me." Sure enough, I found someone with over 300,000 followers and hired him to coach me on what works and what doesn't. At first, it was uncomfortable, but I got the hang of it after a while. Once I became familiar enough with how it worked and what to do, I was able to successfully network on this platform.

- **Meetup Groups:** In October 2017, my wife and I bought our first investment property—a new construction duplex. After signing the contract, I realized it would take forever for us to build wealth by doing duplexes and fourplexes. We had to go *bigger*. I attended a number of local REIA (National Real Estate Investors Association) groups, but they were focused on single-family fix-and-flips. I wanted to build a business with larger-scale multifamily, so I kept searching. One Saturday afternoon, I attended a free multifamily meetup group, where I met a nice couple who shared how they joined a multifamily mentorship group, which helped them get into bigger properties. I said to myself, "If they can do it,

I can do it." It was not cheap for a two-year membership—around $30,000—but I signed up and not once have I ever regretted my decision.

A WISE INVESTMENT

I'm sure many of you reacted in shock at the hefty $30,000 price tag I paid for a two-year membership to a multifamily meetup group. I can hear shouts along the lines of: "Wow—$30K! That's a lot of money!"

For me, it was worth every penny. Joining a multifamily mentorship group adds a lot of value you can't obtain anywhere else. Allow me to share some of the things I gained from having joined Brad Sumrok's group in Dallas, Texas:

- A library of videos discussing each step in the acquisition process
- A private Facebook group, where I could network with other members
- Face-to-face members-only get-togethers
- Events that included both members and non-members
- An Excel spreadsheet to help underwrite and evaluate deals

- A list of several coaches who could schedule time to educate me on any step of the process or discuss the merits of a deal
- Introduction to the other team members and service providers, such as:

    - Property management companies
    - Attorneys
    - Due diligence inspection teams
    - Rehab companies
    - Lenders
    - Brokers

I've been asked many times to identify the greatest value I received. My answer? *The ecosystem.* What do I mean by this? To me, this term refers to the entire pool of trusted contacts I've gained from being part of the group. The ecosystem has given me access to engage business partners who helped me put together deals. I've hired attorneys, property management companies, inspection companies, and general contractors—all from being part of the group. I've met passive investors who want to invest in multifamily deals. I've come across many syndicators who had already done what I set out to accomplish.

Business Relationships

Access to these experts gave me enough confidence to say, "If they can do it, I can do it."

WHAT'S NEXT?

So, you are probably wondering, what happens after you've hired a mentor and achieved the success you were working toward? Look for the next hill to climb. Search for the next goal. Then seek out the best-in-class mentors who can help you get there. I recently saw a saying on social media by Tim Bratz, a seasoned multifamily investor with over 4,000 apartment units, who joined me on my podcast.

> *GOALS*
> *Set 'em up*
> *Knock 'em down.*

Tim recently bought an island. Yes, that's right—an *island*—so I would say he knows what he's writing about. What do you think *his* next hill will be? I don't know, but it will be fun to watch!

Someday, you might be able to have an island of your own. But the first step is to build relationships with investors, business partners, and mentors to build a powerful network of contacts who can help you fulfill your dreams.

Now that you've established a path for building relationships, it's time for you to take on the essential attribute for success most people seem to struggle with the most: *hope.* Is your glass half-full or half-empty? Let's find out.

FIVE

Hope

As I've written earlier in this book, I am a glass half-full kind of guy: an optimist. In general, I believe the world is going to continue to be a better place—not worse. No matter what happens, I am always certain that things will turn out all right and the way they were meant to be. For this reason, I'm focused on the future and the good things that are coming. I have *hope* for a positive future, which I believe is a main contributing factor to my success.

IT WILL WORK OUT FINE

No matter what challenges you may be experiencing, be optimistic and hope for a bright future. We may not be able to predict what unexpected obstacles will get in our way, but focusing on potential negative results won't progress you in life; it will only make you and those around you unhappy and may even lead more directly to those undesired outcomes.

I believe I'm going to live until 100 or more—but who knows when my last day will really come? I choose to live life to the fullest and take smart risks. I am optimistic everything will work out fine.

Many interviewees on my podcast ask themselves, "What's the worst thing that can happen?" if you were to try something new or different. Think about that.

Too many people are held back by fear, which leads to negative thinking. They have multiple ideas, yet don't go after any of them because they are afraid. They remain locked in a dead-end job. I assure you that it doesn't have to be this way. There is always a better way; you just need to believe in yourself. You must figure out what it will take to go after your dream and then pursue it.

Here, I share my views on hope in four different areas:

- Our country
- Our family
- Our finances and business
- Our world

OUR COUNTRY

As I discussed in Chapter Four, I love our country and believe the United States of America is the land of opportunity. That said, there are so many challenges facing our nation, including:

- The political divisions between Democrats and Republicans
- COVID-19 and variants: the worry of loved ones (or yourself) becoming ill and the economic consequences it continues to have on the country as of this writing
- The massive national debt
- Economic threats from other nations, such as China
- Terrorist threats
- Potential stock market and/or real estate market crashes
- Inflation
- Supply chain
- Socioeconomic inequities
- Racial tensions
- Cybercrime

This is by no means even a semi-complete list of America's major concerns! We have a ton of serious problems to grapple with. I'm all in favor of good preparation to manage these circumstances as best as we can, but I'm opposed to wasted time and energy spent being afraid of the worst-case scenario happening, griping about it, and then failing to take the necessary strategic risks.

Here is my response: Stop worrying about what you can't control and focus only on the things you *can* influence in some way. Unless you are a full-time politician or activist, stop posting on social media about politics and reading (and believing) all the propaganda. For example, if you are worried about getting sick or passing the spread of disease, take precautions such as social distancing, mask wearing, and getting vaccinations. If you believe either the stock market or real estate market is overvalued, scale back some of your interests and wait for a pullback.

Here is the caveat: When it comes to reacting to potential business calamities, *always* do your homework first! Rely upon historical evaluations for your decision-making, *never emotions*. Most investors tend to buy when assets keep rising but then panic and sell the moment that prices drop. You need to allow some dry powder to be able to buy more when that panic-selling time comes.

The 2020-2021 financial crisis resulting from the first major wave of COVID-19 was unique in the sense that the stock market plummeted for the first two to three weeks of the shutdown, but then consistently climbed over the subsequent months. If you happened to buy low, you probably doubled your investment in just one year.

Bad stuff will always happen, so it's important to be prepared for them. That said, I would recommend exercising caution when it comes to spending too much time and energy worrying about all the bad things that "could" happen. If you do, you risk missing out on some or all the good things!

The following powerful passage from the Bible (Matthew 6:25–6:27) sums it up well:

> *Therefore I tell you, do not worry about your life, what you will eat or drink; or about your body, what you will wear. Is not life more than food, and the body more than clothes? Look at the birds of the air; they do not sow or reap or store away in barns, and yet your heavenly Father feeds them. Are you not much more valuable than they? Can any one of you by worrying add a single hour to your life?*

FAMILY

I'm a husband, father, son, and uncle.

In the case of my family, as we go through different stages, I'm confident we'll continue to adapt and figure things out as we move forward. Currently, our son is attending college. Our daughter, who graduated from high school this past spring, is taking a year off. As an entrepreneur who believes why not you, I encourage her to go after what she wants in life and not let what others say discourage her. It's her dream. She is determined and persistent, and I believe she can do whatever she puts her mind to. On the other hand, she may decide to start college. I'm good with either path she chooses.

Meanwhile, my wife and I are looking forward to our next stage: empty nesters. We'll probably spend more time traveling and being with one another. I can even imagine later stages when our kids are older and off on their own. They'll begin their careers, get married, and have kids of their own. I'll be a *grandparent*—now *that's* something to look forward to!

What role(s) do you have in your family? Have you thought about each of them in terms of what may or may not happen in the future? Did worrying about things ever help your situation? I doubt it.

Let's take my circumstance, for example. When Tiffany and I were married in Fort Lauderdale, Florida in 1999, we lived in a quaint townhouse. We were still carefree newlyweds, spending most weekends inline skating and/or riding our bikes to the beach. At the time, we didn't have specific plans to start a family. Out of the blue, Tiffany "somehow" became pregnant. Well, we obviously knew *how* it happened, but we weren't ready for it. I admit it: I was *scared*. I didn't know if I was up to being a parent just yet. As each day passed, however, the fear began to subside and was replaced by excitement and anticipation about being a prospective father.

You may already have guessed what happened next: Tragically, Tiffany suffered a miscarriage. We were devastated. After a few weeks went by for us to accept and recover from the loss, we mutually decided to try again as soon as we could. Not long after that, Tiffany became pregnant. Zack was born on September 11, 2000, and Kayla followed on June 20, 2002.

What happened in our case? Once our minds had grasped the concept of parenthood, my wife and I were able to embrace it and look forward to bringing a child into the world. We became confident we would figure it out—no matter what might get in our way. In other words, we developed a tremendous amount of positive hope.

Of all life's commitments, I would say that being a parent is the most difficult—and the most rewarding as well. As parents, we can only do our best. Guaranteed we make mistakes—even with strong advice and warnings from others. You learn as you go. Each stage is a new joy and a fresh challenge. You love your children, you play games with them, you teach them, you cry with them, and you laugh with them. Then, at some point, they grow up and move away and set off on their own journeys. Again, you can only provide them with your wisdom, send them on their way, and hope for the best. They, too, will have their struggles, just as you did. Like you, they will find ways to persevere and succeed.

BUSINESS AND FINANCE

If we can figure out something as complicated as how to start and raise a family, it must be easy to make it in business and achieve our financial goals—right? For many people, *hope* stops at their personal lives; fear takes over when it comes to taking business and financial risks.

As I've stated several times in this book, several real estate investors who joined me on my podcast posed the question: "What's the worst thing that can happen?"

Okay, let's go there for a moment to consider the extreme pessimistic view. Is anyone going to die as a result of a business or financial decision you make? Highly unlikely. At least to my knowledge, no one has lost a life in the multifamily real estate business, for example. With that in mind, you can turn the question "What's the worst thing that can happen?" into even more hopeful ones:

- What have I got to lose?
- What is the best thing that might happen from this decision?
- How will the decision I make impact myself and others short- and long-term?
- What happens if I don't take the risk?
- Is there a tangible and/or intangible cost if I let the opportunity go by?
- How will I feel five years from now if I fail to follow my dream and take the risk? After 10 years? 15 years? 50?

I recently read Academy Award–winning actor Matthew McConaughey's bestselling book *Greenlights*, which is a blend of memoir and personal development. I admit that I was skeptical about it at first. I wasn't sure I was going to like it. As I turned the pages, I became immersed, admiring the calculated risks McConaughey took in his life, many of which paid off *big time* for him.

In one chapter, for example, McConaughey recounts an incident early in his career when he was reading for a side role in a major motion picture, which happened to be an adaptation of John Grisham's thriller *A Time to Kill*. McConaughey did well and was informed he would be great for the part. Instead of simply walking out with a success under his belt, he asked the casting director: "Who do you plan on casting for the lead role alongside Sandra Bullock?"

"I'm not sure," came the reply. "Do you have someone in mind?"

"Yes," he shot back. "*Me*!"

The actor then proceeded to explain why he believed he was perfect for the role. Three or four weeks later, McConaughey received the call asking him to play the male lead. There is no doubt in his mind that this never would have happened if he hadn't made that bold suggestion during the audition. The film, which was released in 1996, catapulted McConaughey's career. Now he is an award-winning actor who has become a household name and has his pick of the best scripts in Hollywood.

OUR WORLD

Earth becomes a smaller place with every passing day. It's faster and easier than ever to connect and communicate with people virtually anywhere in the world with cellphones, social media, and video/phone conferencing. We can exchange images, comments, and stories in seconds. Pandemic-related restrictions aside, we can travel pretty much wherever we want around the world for business and/or pleasure.

This can be a double-edged sword. We are now barraged with bad news from all around the world, not just in terms of what is happening in the United States. Riots, terrorism, pandemics, military conflicts, poverty, famine, disease, nuclear threats, and natural disasters only scratch the surface of what we see and hear from our international news sources and social media friends, who are eager to share the gloom and doom. This bombardment consumes our minds, wastes our time, and holds us hostage out of fear of what may happen.

As solid global citizens who care about people and the fate of our world, what are we to make of this? How can we go about our daily lives when there is so much turmoil in every direction?

If you are passionate about change and committed to doing something about the aforementioned issues (and/or others) as part of your life's mission, I see that as admirable. Go for it! I respect the work of missionaries who circumnavigate the globe preaching the word of God and strive to make our Earth a better place. I applaud individuals who go above and beyond to help bring clean water to unsanitary areas, combat poverty, and educate those who live in places without access to good schools. If you are one of these amazing people, thank you for your contributions. Keep doing what you are doing!

For everyone else out there—which means most people—it's honorable to be worldly and understand the issues facing humankind. At the same time, I know too many people who spend their time fretting over every crisis that arises or what *might* happen and think the world is going to end.

Here's the thing: If you care so much, *do something about it*. Take action—even a small one—to improve the situation. Don't complain about things and then sit on your hands. Once you become involved, believe that you are making a difference and then stay the course.

On various occasions—especially during the events of 9/11—I have heard people say things along the lines of: "How can I bring a child into this world with such a tragedy happening?"

My answer: *love*. Bring a child into the world *to love* him or her. You will make some mistakes along the way and, unfortunately, bad things will continue to show up in the news, but if you focus on just loving and caring for that child, you will understand why I feel so strongly that there is hope in this world.

If you believe our world is heading on the wrong course, become a change agent and feel hopeful that your involvement will make a difference. Become a leader and a role model for the next generations, even if you don't have children (yet). Your efforts will cause a ripple effect and inspire others to follow and learn from you. In turn, they will impact many others to become change agents as well.

HOPE IS NOT A FOUR-LETTER WORD

Always have hope in yourself and the future. *Always* believe that the longshot is possible. *Always* take the risk that will help you fulfill your dream, whatever it may be.

How do you accomplish this? One step at a time. Trust your gut and the pit lodged in your stomach. You might be afraid—so what? It's natural. I'm sure Matthew (McConaughey, not the one from the Bible) had his own set of fears, too, but he *took action* and put himself out there.

Yes, that is the key: *taking action*. The difference between those who achieve their goals and dreams and those who don't is that they side with hope and make a crucial move. They push past their fears. They may fail at first, but the hope lingers, and they press on until they meet with success.

You can do this, too! Once you take a risk and accomplish your goal, you will find you have even greater hope and confidence—along with experience—the next time around and the fears will diminish.

Once again, I urge you to tune out all the negative news from around the world. Instead, fill your mind with positive thoughts. Allow them to encourage you to *take action*. You are on Earth for your individual purpose, but we all have a specific shared purpose as well: to love and help others. The more people you develop relationships with, the more impact you can have on others.

I have hope for the future. I have hope for the country, in my family, and in business and finance. I also have hope that you will overcome your fears and succeed at whatever you happen to be passionate about and then act upon.

As the name of this book says: *Why* Not *You?*

SIX

Learning

Whether you have been in business for five minutes, five years, or five decades, you need to be in a constant state of learning. Invaluable information and solutions have the potential to show up and become implanted in your brain, but you must be on the lookout and ready to open the door to receive this knowledge.

All kinds of content are out there for the taking in the form of books, blogs, magazine and newspaper articles, podcasts, videocasts, and so much more. Soak up everything you can on topics related to your goals. Pick the brains of bona fide experts and incorporate their suggestions into your strategies. Then, of course, you need to *take action*. Once you do so, you will learn even more—from both your successes and mistakes.

Always have the courage to believe in yourself and make a decision, one way or the other. Whether the outcome is positive or negative, you will learn from the result. Trust me when I say this: For the most part, you are going to be glad that you made your decisions. Afterward, you will likely say, "I should have done this or that before I made my decision. But you know what? Next time, I'll do better."

Every successful entrepreneur is in a constant state of learning. Each such individual may have a different preference when it comes to his or her favored source—whether it's books, interviews with people, podcasts, or blogs—but is willing to admit when he or she does not know something and then takes pains to fill those gaps. The most successful people have curious minds and constantly seek answers and new directions regarding their passions.

In this chapter, we are going to review five areas that were of great interest to me:

1. Multifamily investing
2. Personal wealth management
3. Social media
4. How to start a podcast
5. How to start a YouTube channel

What do *you* need to learn to drive your business and further your personal growth and development?

ENTERING MULTIFAMILY INVESTING

I started my journey in learning by reviewing Realtor.com for duplexes in the DFW (Dallas–Fort Worth) area. Since this was going to be my first real estate investment outside of my personal residence, I wanted to start small.

I took small steps to find my footing. I found a new construction duplex for sale a couple of towns away from where I lived. Next, I toured a similar property in the area. I followed that up by hiring an attorney to review the purchase contract. I subsequently met with local banks to discuss loan options. I called property management companies to find someone to manage the property after closing. I ran the numbers to ensure I would be cash flow positive once the deal was done.

Here's the thing. I had plenty of capital to do the deal but faced a major problem: I was *still scared*. Despite all my research and due diligence, I remained unsure of whether I had paid a good price for the property. Not only that, I felt unsure of how it was going to turn out after the ink was dry. I was accustomed to trading large loan portfolios in which the buyer and seller negotiated the purchase and sale agreement. While buying the duplex, we submitted redlines of the purchase agreement, but the seller refused to modify the agreement. Not a single change was accepted.

When I asked my attorney, she said it was completely up to me. I had to know what risks I was taking if I were to conclude the deal, so I consulted with a relative who had been involved in large real estate transactions. He told me that he wouldn't do it if he were in my place. He posed this question: "What will you do if the economy goes south, and the builder runs out of money to complete the construction?"

We attempted to insert some language in the agreement to protect us against such a circumstance. Naturally, the seller rejected this change, too.

I had an important decision to make. Should I pass on the deal or move forward with the lopsided contractual language? If I declined, I would never know if it would work or not and possibly miss out on a lucrative opportunity. If I signed the deal and it failed because one of my agreement requests had been refused, I would lose a lot of money and feel like a fool.

What should I do?

After much deliberation, I caved in and signed the agreement. Why? Because I came to the realization that I would *learn* something, whether the deal ended up being successful or not.

Shortly after I signed the agreement, I realized it was going to take a long time to build wealth going from duplex to fourplex to eightplex, etc., so I searched for a way to grow.

How can I get involved in even larger deals? How will I learn to do a large-scale multifamily investment?

The duplex with the lousy contract turned out to be exactly what I needed. If I hadn't purchased it, I wouldn't have even been able to consider going even bigger. Learning while taking action leads you to places you didn't even know existed. It starts the ball rolling. I own that duplex to this very day. It provides strong cash flow, and similar properties in the area have appreciated in value. If we were to sell it now, we would realize a nice positive gain. The most important part, however, was how that purchase led me to go bigger and chase my next goal.

Another benefit of the duplex deal was that it led to my searching for investment groups. The first meetings I attended focused on single-family fix-and-flips, which was not what I was looking for. So, I kept searching. Finally, one Saturday, I found a free group meeting focused on multifamily investing that took place at a restaurant about 45 minutes from my house.

I must admit, I was nervous. I assumed these people had a lot more knowledge and experience than I did. What if I were to become so intimidated that I couldn't summon enough confidence to introduce myself to people and ask them questions? What if they were unfriendly and/or held back the important stuff I really needed to know?

As it turned out, attending the meeting was a wise decision. I mustered enough courage to approach some of the approximately 20 people there and ask questions. The first couple was super nice and shared their story with me, which had many similarities to mine. They were business owners who wanted to ramp up their investing. They knew they wanted to do it with multifamily but, at first, couldn't figure out how to get involved. They joined a multifamily mentorship group, which provided the answers. They went on to earn a lot of money for themselves and their investors. None of this would have happened if they hadn't joined the mentorship group. I was so impressed with their story that I signed up with the mentorship group that week, in December 2017.

My first step was to set up meetings at Starbucks with a bunch of sponsors or general partners in the group over the course of the next several weeks. I wanted to find out as soon as possible if this was "real" or not. I picked their brains on multifamily investing, and they were more than happy to share their knowledge and answer my questions. It didn't take long for me to realize how genuine these wealth-building opportunities were and that they had endless potential. One of these sponsors asked me to guess his net worth. I speculated $9 million. He responded by saying he was north of that.

It took nine months from when I began with the group to be awarded my first syndication deal and a few months after that to close it. In total, it was about a year from start to finish before I was officially through the door. From there, I went from a duplex to a 76-unit townhome community.

It's amazing what you can accomplish once you believe in yourself and become involved with the right people. I am so thankful to those who helped me along the way and hope this story will inspire you to follow suit and go after your dreams and goals.

MASTERING PERSONAL WEALTH MANAGEMENT

Once I became involved with a multifamily mentorship group, I met many seasoned real estate investors. Not only did they impart to me their knowledge of how to invest in multifamily properties, they recommended books, offered personal advice, and shared their informative stories.

One evening, while at a networking event, an investor suggested I read the book *Tax-Free Wealth*, by Tom Wheelwright. I ordered it the following day and started reading as soon as it arrived. While flipping the pages, I felt like I was in church, and the pastor was speaking directly to me. Have you ever felt that way while reading a book? I was especially taken by Wheelwright's statement that many people believe it's the patriotic duty of every American to pay their fair share of taxes. I couldn't agree with him more.

The author next goes on to explain that the tax code is several thousand pages long. The first few pages outline how, if you happen to be a W-2 employee (a typical worker receiving a salary), and make $XX income, then you pay $YY in taxes. It's as simple as that.

The remainder of the tax code consists of government incentives to encourage citizens to invest in certain industries, such as affordable housing. I thought to myself, *Why haven't I taken the time to learn about these tax incentives?*

I read through Wheelwright's book, conferred with other experts, and finally started to see the big picture. The government provides tax incentives for investors to purchase and/or invest in real estate. When capital funnels into these apartment properties, they become cleaner and safer, while still being affordable to renters.

Another thing I learned from fellow real estate investors: sources of capital. I was happy to discover, for example, that I could use retirement funds to invest in multifamily deals. In addition, I realized that I could transfer funds from my existing IRA or SEP-IRA (a Simplified Employee Pension Individual Retirement Account) into one of three types of accounts:

1. Self-directed IRA (SDIRA, which allows alternative investments for retirement savings)
2. Solo 401(k) (a retirement plan for business owners who don't have full-time employees other than themselves and their spouses)
3. Qualified retirement plan (QRP, a pension plan in which self-employed workers can defer taxes to plan for retirement)

This all sounded complicated at first, but then I figured out that it's a simple rollover from my existing IRA into one of these new accounts. Once I started doing it, the transaction felt like a rollover of a 401(k) plan from a former employer into an IRA. The main difference in this instance is that, once the funds are in this new account, I have the choice of many investment options, not just the stock market.[1]

I also found out that I could leverage the equity in my home for an investment. This made as much sense to me then as it does now, but everyone has his or her own comfort level on the subject. My advice is that you always stick to your gut and do what feels right. Some people are focused on paying off their mortgage and like to have peace of mind about not having to make a monthly payment. This may be the right way to go for some people, given their circumstances and personal preferences. As for me, I am perfectly fine being able to leverage equity to own more cash-flowing assets.

---

[1] *Note:* Make sure you consult your CPA and tax advisor before making any decision on which account to set up. There are also tax implications to consider. SDIRAs are subject to UBIT taxes (Unrelated Business Income Tax), which can amount to thousands of dollars, whereas Solo 401(k)s and QRPs are not subject to such tax.

If you choose to leverage your home equity, there are a few ways you can access the funds for this purpose:

1. Obtain a cash-out refinance (after refinancing a home, the homeowner receives cash at closing)
2. File for a home equity line of credit
3. Sell your home and rent living space

In December 2019, my wife and I chose option #3 from the above. Our oldest son was in college and our daughter was heading into her senior year. Tiffany and I were unsure of where we were going to spend our empty nester years, so selling our house, renting, and investing the capital from the sale of our home into multifamily cash-flowing properties made sense. As it happens, the COVID pandemic broke out three months later, and we felt as if we'd gotten out just in time. Currently, housing prices have skyrocketed so, if we'd held off another year, we would have made a much greater profit. Hindsight is 20/20.

If you happen to have young children, your home is much more than a place to live and possible investment. It's where you create life memories. It has sentimental value. For these reasons alone, you might not be ready to sell. Keep in mind that it's possible to keep your house and still leverage the equity you built up in it by doing a cash-out refinance or home equity line of credit.

Let's walk through an example: A family has a $500K home they purchased in 2015 with 20 percent down or $100K. Flash forward to the present, it's now worth $700K, so the couple now has $300K equity in the house ($100K original down payment, plus the $200K increase in value)—their one asset. They still reside in it, so they do not receive any positive cash flow. They are paying the mortgage each month, which means they have negative cash flow; however, the asset has the potential to appreciate each year.

Let's suppose the couple looks into getting a cash-out refinance at a 75 percent loan to value (LTV, the percentage of loan you can obtain based on the value of the property)—which amounts to a $525K loan. Their original loan was $400K and, over the past seven years, there would be principal paydown. For simplicity, let's just focus on the $125K in cash that this couple could leverage. Let's assume the mortgage rates are 3 percent. The couple could invest in a multifamily property with projected annual distributions of 7 percent. Assuming these distributions occur as projected, the couple would be cash flow positive and own two assets.

Can things potentially go wrong with this approach? Absolutely! I've invested in numerous multifamily properties; some of them have made distributions as projected, while others haven't. Even those that were light on distributions still managed to provide a significant return upon sale.

Before deciding what you would like to do, analyze your situation and be realistic. If the distributions don't materialize as planned, can you still easily afford the larger mortgage payment? If not, then another investment—such as acting as a hard money lender—may be a better option.

My intention is not to suggest that the same investment option will work for every situation. Instead, I encourage you to learn and understand all the options available, if you are looking to invest and need enough capital to make it work.

The main point here is that many of us have access to unused capital. Equity in our home is one example. Retirement funds in IRAs, SEPs, and 401(k)s are another. It is estimated that the total value of homeowner equity in the United States is $21 trillion as of 2020 and $12 trillion sitting in retirement accounts as of 2021. That's a massive amount of capital available to invest!

GETTING INVOLVED IN SOCIAL MEDIA

Prior to joining the multifamily mentorship group, I didn't have much of a social media footprint. I wasn't on Facebook, Twitter, YouTube, or Instagram. LinkedIn was the extent of it and, even in that case, I didn't do much in the way of engagement and outreach. Once I became part of the mentorship group, it seemed safe and easy for me to join their private Facebook group. One immediate benefit was that I was able to exchange direct messages with other members. This led to some useful online chats and occasional phone conversations. Finally, I began to see the upside of social media as a way to connect with like-minded people from all over the country (and, later, around the world).

I remember attending a bunch of entrepreneurial conferences, during which several attendees stressed to me the importance of being on Instagram. At the time, I didn't understand it at all; I thought it was just an app on which kids could post pictures, and I didn't feel any need to create a profile. After a while, so many people told me I had to have an Instagram account that I attended a conference for the sole purpose of determining its value and finding a capable person to manage it for me. I found just the right expert and hired him on the spot.

It seems silly looking back on it, but I admit that at the time I didn't even know how to set up an Instagram account and profile. Once he helped me accomplish that, he showed me the ropes and told me that I had to post every day.

Every day? I thought. *What am I going to post about? How will people react to my posts?*

I was so nervous about my first post that I struggled clicking the post button. Naturally, I had nothing to fear. The post was an immediate hit, and people from all over—from Chicago to Las Vegas—wanted to connect with me. Some even asked to speak by phone. To my surprise, quite a few wanted to learn from my experiences. I was more than happy to share my knowledge with them. After all, others had done the same for me.

Once again, I witnessed the power of social media and its ability to connect people. Yes, at first it was challenging and uncomfortable, but once you get accustomed to it, you realize that this is a way to share and give back to the community, as well as continue to learn and grow yourself.

STARTING A PODCAST

Back in February 2020, I was working hard on a 200+ unit deal in the DFW area. I put a lot of time and effort into the project and thought for sure I was going to win it. My group came in second, which is the same as finishing last. There are no runner-up prizes in multifamily investing. If you lose, you lose.

It would be an understatement to say that I was bummed. I knew I had to work through the loss and quickly come to terms with it so, a couple of days later, I focused on figuring out how I could rebound. I asked God, *Okay, what's next? Should I go after my next deal?*

The answer came to me in the form of a whisper: *podcast.*

There was no reason on earth for me to have thought about podcasting at that moment. I had included it on my list of goals for the year—but it was *way down* in terms of priority. At the time, I figured I would tackle it at the end of the year (if at all). I took out my phone and Googled "podcast conferences."

As fortune would have it, Podfest—a community of people who meet several times a year for two or three days to discuss and learn about audio and video broadcasting—was taking place in Florida the following week. I immediately bought a ticket and booked my hotel.

I didn't have a clue about what I was going to do once I arrived at the event. I didn't know a thing about podcasting and certainly didn't know anyone who would be attending. Once again, I was throwing myself in the deep end of the pool. On my way there, I wondered whether I was wasting my time and money and, worse, if I was going to embarrass myself in front of everyone with my lack of knowledge.

My outlook brightened when I attended various beginner sessions. I met some great people there and no one made me feel uncomfortable. I learned many things, including:

1. Equipment I needed to purchase
2. The fact that everyone starts raw and improves over time
3. It is crucial to leverage other people who have more experience.

In addition, I met a podcasting expert who ultimately became my consultant. Another session leader recommended I read *Start with Why*, by Simon Sinek. This bestseller helped me focus on *why* I was starting this podcast and *whom* it would be meant to serve. I concluded that I had a two-fold *why*:

1. I want to grow my family's wealth. This podcast would be a way to attract new investors and business partners.
2. I want to inspire others to go after their dreams and goals.

Prior to going to the Podfest conference, I participated as a guest on several other people's podcasts, including *Evan Holladay's Monumental Podcast*. After Evan and I completed the recording, I asked him whether he found value in doing his podcast show. He explained how the podcast had opened so many doors for him. He went on to suggest that I read *Subscribe, Rate & Review*, by Carson Jones. I bought it right away and finished it in a few days. This book outlined all the steps and considerations I would need to consider when starting a podcast. It gave me a solid foundation on what to expect, after which I leaned on my consultant to provide guidance and advice along the way.

Having gained all this knowledge, it was time to put it into practice and start the podcast. I enjoyed it from the get-go. I love getting DMs (direct messages) from people telling me they learned a lot from listening. But I don't view it as being all about me imparting wisdom to other people. Like my listeners, I also learn a great deal from my guests.

In this way, the podcast has helped fill in my *why:* It drives investors and business partners to me and inspires my listeners to go out and follow their dreams. That is what learning is all about.

LAUNCHING A YOUTUBE CHANNEL

It seems only natural that a podcast would lead to a videocast, the largest platform being, of course, YouTube. My foray into video began when I attended a Mastermind group of about 30 people in Jamaica. Among the attendees was Rod Khleif, the host of *The Lifetime CashFlow Through Real Estate Podcast*, who had been one of the inspirations for my own podcast. It was an honor meeting him, and I was thrilled at having the opportunity to ask him for advice in person. One of the things he suggested to me was publishing the podcast on YouTube.

The thought had occurred to me. But once again I didn't know how to make it happen and was initially scared to put the videos out there.

What if nobody watches?

I researched everything I could about YouTube and began posting videos on the channel in the first quarter of 2021. Since then, I have published over 60 video podcast episodes, a whole bunch of podcast clips, and an assortment of podcast audiograms containing short highlights or summaries.

In a nutshell, if I can do podcasts and videocasts, anything is possible for you—as long as you do the research and learn from the best on how to do the task professionally. Instead of just "winging it," you want to consult with people who have "been there and done that" to save yourself the headaches and lost time and money on what might end up being poorly conceived and executed products. You would be amazed by how many authorities are out there who are more than willing to help. All you need to do is search them out and ask!

While you want to be super-confident about yourself and your abilities, always be willing to admit when you don't know something and seek counsel. Asking questions is a sign of strength, not weakness. Nobody expects you to know everything right out of the gate. The key to success in any new endeavor is to *have an open mind* and *be willing to learn*. Then the fun really begins!

SEVEN

Work Hard

Throughout this book, I have used the words *work hard*. What do I mean by them?

I believe in the 80/20 rule, whereby 20 percent of the people rise up and find a way to be successful and the other 80 percent just coast. I want you to be part of the 20 percent who succeed beyond their wildest imaginations. How do you go about doing this?

There are many stories of individuals who, on the surface, seem to have been overnight successes. In reality, most of them worked extremely hard over a number of years to get to that point. They plowed through the setbacks and failures without receiving any rewards or recognition for their blood, sweat, and tears. Then, seemingly out of nowhere, their time finally arrived, and a breakthrough occurred. Maybe they met the right person at the right time who opened a door for them. Perhaps they met with some other unexpected stroke of luck. Or something they have been percolating for many years all came together after years of development. To the outsider, this seems like overnight success. For them—and perhaps a few insiders—the memories of the hard work remain fresh. And yet, through all the disappointments, they made sacrifices and persevered, preparing themselves for the special moment when they made it over the top. They had one thing that many people seem to lack—and I don't mean intelligence, creativity, or skill. I'm referring to one thing: *grit*. They put in the *hard work*.

Everyone has a different starting point. Some people have the capital to set up shop right away. Others need to tighten their belts and find ways to get by—such as building the business in the evenings and on weekends while working somewhere that pays the bills—until revenue starts coming in. In some industries, seed money from investors is essential. There is no right or wrong starting point. You must believe in your vision, passion, and goals with all your heart and soul. Some people might not see it and will try to shoot you down and convince you that you are wasting your time. Don't listen to them! Keep pushing forward anyway. If you don't, you will be validating the naysayers without giving your dream a chance to breathe and take flight.

This conjures up the story of J. K. Rowling. Some people think she was an overnight success; however, she was far from it. Before she sold her first book, she was an unemployed single mom[2] suffering from clinical depression. She regarded herself as a failure and even considered taking her own life. Her pitch to publishers for her first Harry Potter book was rejected by a dozen publishers before Bloomsbury took a chance on it. In 1997, they printed 500 hardcover copies of[3] *Harry Potter and the Philosopher's Stone.*

Many years later, Rowling has written nearly 20 books and sold *more than half a billion copies* worldwide.[4] Her Harry Potter series is the bestselling series of all time. Overnight success? Not so much. Unlike many people who give up, she pressed on when the world was telling her *No.*

---

[2] Source: https://observer.com/2017/04/j-k-rowling-how-to-deal-with-failure/
[3] Source: https://www.bloomsbury.com/uk/discover/harry-potter/harry-potter-fun-stuff/a-potted-history-of-harry-potter/
[4] Source: https://www.wizardingworld.com/news/500-million-harry-potter-books-have-now-been-sold-worldwide

Another major example: The Beatles—the most influential rock band in the world—were turned away by every record label in London before they finally landed a contract. They famously failed their audition with Decca Records. It wasn't until producer George Martin at Parlophone/EMI saw something special and took a chance signing them to a recording contract. That only happened after the group had put in thousands of hours sweating it out and honing their craft in grungy clubs across England and Germany.

As you know by now, I attend many entrepreneurial events and real estate conferences. I love to learn from others. One such event was an intimate, three-day get-together among 30 people at Dr. Greg Reid's (coauthor of *Three Feet from Gold* and author of *Wealth Made Easy*) home. At a certain point during the event, he led the entire group upstairs to an area I can best describe as a loft-like living room.

Oddly, Greg picked up a basket and dumped its contents on the floor right in front of us. The group stared at the mess of envelopes and letters.

What is he doing? What's the significance of this? we wondered.

"These are all of the rejection letters I received on my first book," he announced.

The group stared in disbelief. There had to have been at least fifty letters in that pile.

In the years that passed since Greg received all those rejections, he has authored and/or coauthored around 80 books, nearly half of which have been bestsellers. Greg's point? Like J. K. Rowling, he dug deep and found a way to believe in himself and press onward.

It's never easy for Dr. Reid, The Beatles, J. K. Rowling, or anyone else, including me. It takes enormous strength to follow your path when all the signals around you are negative and telling you to stop. All the while, your submerged inner voice is desperate to be heard and ask, *Who cares? What do they know? We have to keep going. Our goals and dreams are too important to us to throw in the towel now.*

The funny thing is, at first your goal or ambition might be a selfish one but, once you accomplish it, everyone cheers you on, congratulates you, and asks, "How did you do it?" When you share your success story, you inspire and motivate others to also take action (which we will fully explore in the final chapter).

"Huh," they'll say to themselves, "If *he* can do it, I'm sure I could, too!"

VISUALIZE TO MOTIVATE HARD WORK

Visualize what you want to be in one, three, five, and even 10 years. Write down these ambitions and lock them in your mind. Create a Vision Board to help you picture your success. You can do this on any kind of poster board, and it doesn't have to be a work of art. Simply depict what your vision looks like down the road. You can draw objects or cut-and-paste images or photographs onto the board. (For example, an actor might include photographs of Kevin Costner, Denzel Washington, Julia Roberts, Will Smith, Sandra Bullock, and Jack Nicholson, along with a picture of the famous Hollywood sign on the hills in Los Angeles.)

Another way to reinforce your vision is to record a narrative of it and listen to it every day. Again, it doesn't need to be a professional recording with sound effects or even be that lengthy. A two-minute audio clip of your voice on your phone would suffice.

Once you have completed all of this, make a commitment to do the hard work that will make it all happen.

As I said before: This isn't going to be easy. That's why you need to drill deep inside yourself to find what is most important to you. God created all of us as unique; every one of us has different goals and dreams. We all have individual ways of doing things. Even in a crowded industry, there is plenty of room for entrepreneurial people to break in and find their niche.

It's entirely possible you haven't found the right team of people to work with yet who share your goals, passion, ideals, and work style. It's unusual to luck into making those connections right away. Be patient. Your people are out there. You will seek out some of them, whereas others will seem to miraculously appear when you least expect it. Your odds decrease, however, if you haven't visualized where you are headed. How can you expect to have others join you on your journey if you haven't yet determined where you are going?

PASSION FUELS THE WORK ENGINE

Once you have completed your visualization, identify your *true passion*. Give this as much thought as you can. What do you love to do? What is driving you forward when things get tough? What is grumbling in the pit of your stomach?

Passion is the essential fuel that keeps you going through the ups and downs. Without it, you'll give up without even fully trying. I'm not being negative when I say bad things will probably happen along your journey. It's just the reality. Some projects will go south and fail, whether the outcome is within your control or not. If you have enough passion running your engine, you will pick yourself right up and keep going, having learned some things along the way that will guide you the next time around.

BREAK DOWN YOUR GOALS

Once you have identified your vision and passion, you need to break down the goals you must complete to turn your dream into reality. This is where the *hard work* comes in. There may be items on this list you don't like to do, which is to be expected. You can't skip over or race through them. You have to get these things done correctly, so you have a foundation on which to build your business. Don't worry, you'll get to the fun stuff later.

Picture an athlete that you admire. In your mind, you see a perfect specimen who has accomplished many great things. Do you think about how many hours that athlete put in at the gym to get in such magnificent shape, or do you visualize that great touchdown catch he made or soccer goal she scored? Naturally, it's the spectacular feat that stays with you. But that accomplishment would not have been possible if the athlete hadn't made concrete goals and put in the hours of arduous hard work and training.

Don't worry about whether your goals seem to be unattainable and on a road that goes on forever. Once you accomplish one goal, you set another one that's even greater. You continue to complete one after the other, until you reflect back, look at everything you've done, and realize how far you have come. With those successes in your rearview mirror, you can pave the way for another series of seemingly impossible goals. But you know you will conquer them because you have been successful in the past.

Over the years, I've interviewed real estate investors who have owned thousands of multifamily units. The common denominator? They all started with a *first property*. Usually, though not always, it started with a single-family home, but sometimes it was a duplex or even a multifamily. Whatever the case, everyone begins somewhere and goes from zero properties to one, then another, and then another. That's all you need in the beginning: one block to build on. The rest will follow.

If any of your goals seem too challenging for you to figure out on your own, refer back to Chapter Six and think about how you will go about obtaining that missing knowledge. This also becomes a key goal.

MY INSPIRATIONS FOR WORKING SO HARD

Mine is not a rags-to-riches story. My grandfather was a successful entrepreneur who owned a scrap aluminum company in Connecticut, where I grew up. My dad worked for the company and climbed up the ranks until he became president, a role he held for many years.

My dad liked to travel in style, so when heading off on vacation he'd pick me up from school in a limo to drive us to the airport. Most people would regard that as being pretty cool. Not me. I didn't like the attention, nor did I want to appear to have more money than anyone else. Other kids assumed I was fed with a golden spoon and had it easy; someday, they thought, I'd land a cushy job in the family business.

I didn't want any of that. I refused to have success handed to me. I wanted to find it my own way. I may not have always known how to do it, but I always believed I could—and *would*—do it.

Follow your own path. Don't let your friends, family, coworkers, teachers, social media community, or anyone else dictate what you should and shouldn't do. Trust your gut, decide, commit, put a plan in place, and then execute it. Always remember this quote from the Gospel of Matthew 19:26 (which is also Ohio's state motto)[5]: "With God, all things are possible."

My journey to where I am now hasn't always been a straight line. But that's okay. For me, it's always been about the overall journey, not the pit stops along the way. In each of my career roles, I was focused and determined to be the best I could be.

The first thing that motivates me as a real estate investor is building wealth that provides *financial freedom* and *freedom of time*. Secondly, I am driven by the desire and ability to help and serve others. When you buy large apartment communities, you are typically pooling together capital from many different families. As you help grow the valuation of the property, you are contributing

---

[5] Source: https://ohio.gov/wps/portal/gov/site/government/resources/state-symbols

wealth for the families invested in the deal. You are also improving the physical condition of the property, which positively impacts the tenants who live there.

Below I will share with you three personal examples of working hard that will hopefully resonate with you.

Kindergarten Guest Speaker

When I was in kindergarten, we had a guest speaker visit the class. The students filed into the school library and sat cross-legged on the carpet in silence. The speaker shared a story about two brothers: one was always getting into trouble; the other was focused and successful. The siblings were asked the same question: "Why do you think you ended up where you did?"

Both answered the same way: "Our father was an alcoholic."

This story has nothing to do with my family, yet it is a simple story that struck a chord for me that has remained with me for many years. The point I gleaned—both then and now—is that everyone faces difficulties. People may have shared the same experience, yet one uses it as an excuse for his/her shortcomings, whereas the other turns the situation into a motivating factor that guides him/her toward achieving success.

I firmly believe that entrepreneurs can only succeed by working hard and making their own way, not using obstacles to defend failure.

Laps Around the Tennis Court

Back in high school, I was one of the captains of the football team. There was one occasion during the summer when I had to stay home, causing me to miss a practice. Instead of enjoying being off the hook and not having to do grueling exercise that day, I became determined to make up for it on my own. I went out to the tennis court and began to run laps. Although I had no concept of how long one lap around the court was, I decided to run 100 of them. I didn't consider whether it would be easy or hard; I just ran.

After having completed just a few dozen laps, I realized I had overestimated my goal. This was *really difficult*. I wanted to quit. Nobody was watching, so what difference would it have made?

And yet . . . it *did* make a difference—*to me*. *I'd* know. I had to prove to myself that this is what a real captain — the team leader—would do. So, I kept going through the sweat, muscle aches, cramps, and exhaustion. I completed my goal, even though no one was there to take notice.

I have a few points in telling this story. The first is that hard work is always going to be about yourself. People won't always be around to cheer you on. Sometimes, you do tough things even when no one is around for encouragement and support or to give you a pat on the back.

Secondly, that story remains fresh in my mind as a stored reminder for me to always work hard, do my best, and never give up when starting something new and challenging. Once you build up a success story—even a minor one, such as running laps—you have it locked in your memory for the next time and every single one after that. It will remind you that you are capable of persevering—no matter what—because you beat the odds in the past.

Getting My Act Together in College

Like many college students past and present, I goofed off during my freshman year. This resulted in a sub-3.0 GPA, which I admit embarrassed me. For my sophomore year, I resolved to turn things around. I set my sights on achieving a high GPA in my major, accounting, that would boost my resume later on.

I tried studying in several different locations on campus to find out which one would produce the best result:

my room, study rooms, the university library, and others. I spent time by myself, in study groups, and with other people hanging out. I compared how well I did at different times of the day as well.

After some trial and error, I concluded that a certain tiny cubicle on the quietest floor of the library—the top one, in fact—was where I could truly focus. I created a routine of studying in this spot every evening at about the same time. It seemed to do the trick, as I was able to sit there for hours straight until I knew the material.

I completed my four years with a cumulative GPA of around 3.0. However, my *accounting* GPA reached 3.72. Naturally, that's what I noted on my resume, which was enough to land my first job offer, at PriceWaterhouse. I was thrilled—all those hours spent hunched in a library cubicle alone and in silence had paid off.

DAILY ROUTINES

One of the many great books I've read over the years is *The Slight Edge: Turning Simple Disciplines into Massive Success and Happiness*, by Jeff Olson. The author offers a method of processing information that enables you to make the daily choices that will lead you to attain the success and happiness you desire. This ability is what separates the people who make their dreams come true from those who just keep on dreaming. Olson's premise is simple: If you do tasks consistently every day, that effort will accumulate over time and give you an edge.

While I try to follow Olson's method, I admit I'm not perfect. There are times when I've lost focus and strayed from my routines. However, I've found that I feel better, accomplish more, and produce better work when I stick to consistent routines.

Below are a few of my most effective routines. I'm not suggesting you literally do the same ones, but rather, use them as examples to help create your own daily regimens.

1. *Read a Bible chapter* in the *morning*. Initially, I had kept my Bible in the nighttable next to my bed, as many people do. The routine didn't stick, and it was easy for me to figure out why. Although I wanted to read every morning when I woke up, I couldn't even get myself to open the nighttable drawer. The location and timing didn't work for me. I decided to move the Bible into my office and place it on my desk as a visual

reminder. With the Bible front and center and in my workspace, I was able to focus on it and read a chapter in the morning. A simple step such as moving the activity can sometimes make a big difference.

2. *Post on Instagram every day.* You may recall in the last chapter that a social media authority urged me to post every single day. I struggled with this at first, not knowing if I would have something to say on a daily basis. I decided to try it first thing every morning to get it out of the way. Sure enough, this clicked, and I began posting every morning like clockwork.

3. *Accomplish the one or two tasks that will bring you closest to achieving your goals.* This is a tip I picked up in Brian Tracy's book *Eat That Frog!* Instead of focusing on the little things—the busywork—and checking boxes as "complete" but barely moving the needle, tackle the *biggest, most important ones* first. The more you avoid working on these goals, the more you allow time to slip away from accomplishing your dreams. Waiting until you are "in the right mood" and procrastinating ends up making these goals seem even more daunting.

4. *Read quality business books.* Books have always played a major role in my work and personal life. Here are two shining examples:

    - Years ago, when I started working on a bank trading floor, I began my day by going to Starbucks at 5:00 or 6:00 a.m. I would bring with me a monster-sized book on trading mortgage-backed securities. Though the book's topic was complicated, it turned out to be well worth the effort; it was filled with information that I directly applied to my job and gave me an edge.

    - Shortly after I started my podcast, I sent a text to a contact I'd met at a conference in the hope I would bring him on as a guest. He may not have been a billionaire, but he was close—in the neighborhood of $700 million. Soon after I sent the text, my phone rang and . . . it was him! I thought this was a great sign that he was prepared to appear on my podcast. Unfortunately, the conversation didn't go that way. Instead, he told me to read *Maximum*

Achievement, another book by Brian Tracy. I bought it right away and read it over the weekend. I called my wealthy acquaintance to thank him for the recommendation. I told him I thought it was a great book and that it had already inspired an idea—creating an audio file of my goals to supplement my Vision Board (described earlier in this chapter). The point is this: While we may think we are too busy to read business books, it is *essential* that you do it to get expert advice. There is no doubt you will find each one inspiring with at least one important takeaway—and perhaps a breakthrough idea as well.

WORK/LIFE BALANCE

While I encourage you to work hard, create opportunities, and push through obstacles and setbacks, I believe it's equally as important for you to pay attention to the people you love and care about, especially family and friends. What good is a healthy mind and body and a large account balance if you've ignored people so much that no one is around to be with you when you are 90?

Here are my thoughts on priorities for maintaining strong work/life balance:

1. Relationship with the Big Man upstairs
2. Personal relationships—family and friends
3. Relationship with your body and staying healthy and in shape
4. Relationships with business partners, associates, workers, clients, and customers

Your devotion to these four priorities will make you wealthy in more ways than you can possibly imagine. *Never ever* sacrifice the quality of any of these areas. Making money is important but should not be prioritized over these four.

I once saw a poster in an office that read something along the lines of: "Success is not easy, but it's worth it!"

In other words, *always put in the hard work*. Don't worry, you've got this!

EIGHT

The Ability to Create Wealth

It's a shame how most people learn about money. We are mostly taught how to be *employees*, rather than leaders, owners, and entrepreneurs. Teachers and parents encourage us to land the best paying job and climb the corporate ladder to earn more W-2 income. What they don't explain is that W-2 earnings are taxed by the government at the highest rates, which means you won't have as much opportunity to create long-term wealth.

If you haven't yet read *Rich Dad Poor Dad*, by Robert T. Kiyosaki, now is the time to find a copy and open it up to page one. It's a must read for everyone. In the book, Kiyosaki outlines the various ways you can earn money and what the tax rates are for each category. The wealthy get wealthier because they understand that it's not about how much money they make, but rather, how they generate income and how it will be taxed. In other words, it's *what you keep after taxes that is most important.*

If you haven't learned this philosophy up until now, don't worry: There is still plenty of time. I didn't figure it out either until I became involved in the real estate investing industry about four years ago. Since I developed an awareness and understanding of how it works, it has had a massive positive impact on my finances, which I will share with you.

SAFETY AND SECURITY

Time and time again, I've heard people repeat the mantra that having a job "provides security." Sure, it's nice knowing that you have a steady paycheck coming in. Stability sounds like a fine concept and feels good in terms of having enough to pay the bills every month. However, things don't necessarily play out that way in the real world. Allow me to offer a couple of personal stories to demonstrate what I mean.

What's Left to Show After Years of Service
While I was in my 20s, I worked for a large software company selling accounting software to Fortune 1000

companies. I considered my boss a cool guy. Both he and his wife had been with the company for many years and did well for themselves. While he ran the sales division for the enterprise software applications, his wife did the same for the other parts of the organization. The couple had no qualms about working long hours or separating for long periods of business travel. Their biggest sacrifice, left unsaid, was that they never had any children. While there may have been other reasons for this that were unknown to me, I personally believe work was the main factor; they had chosen to climb up the corporate ladder, rather than raise a family.

Let me tell you: My boss seemed incredibly happy with his career and the general state of things. He had a positive outlook and always offered to help those around him who needed it. I saw it as a privilege to work with someone who was willing to share his enormous knowledge and have such a generous heart supporting others.

One day, all of that changed. The company decided to give his wife's position to a younger person who worked in the company. They kept her on, but she was basically shoved aside and into a reduced, less-important role.

My boss did not take well to the company's treatment of his wife. The money they had earned over the years did not make up for what he regarded as lack of appreciation for her years of loyal service. It also wasn't worth the sacrifice they made, choosing to put in time for the company over building a family.

The couple eventually retired with a perfectly adequate nest egg. I sensed, however, that the experience with the company left resentment and a bitter taste in their mouths. Their prime years, which they had dedicated to the company, felt wasted.

Witnessing this story unfold taught me a lesson. There is little-to-no loyalty to workers in Corporate America. It's all about "What have you done for me lately?" The days of spending 20 or 30 years with a company and then receiving a bon voyage party at the end with a gold watch are long gone. I did not feel any sense of stability or security watching how this couple was treated. Instead, I realized that everyone is in it for him or herself. The gist of this is that employees should learn as much as they can with their employers to make themselves as marketable as possible for their next, more rewarding role up the ladder. The longer they stay, the more these companies will wring out of them to make the greatest profit possible for themselves.

If you feel underpaid and underappreciated working for someone else now, imagine how you will feel 10, 20, or 30 years down the road after you have job-hopped from one company to the next, hoping each one will be better and more fulfilling. What will all this work have brought you and your family? Will you be rich and happy? What sacrifices did you make along the way that you regret?

I encourage you to mull over these questions as we dive into the second story.

The Reality for At-Will Employees

Venkat Avasarala, a cofounder of Raven Multifamily whom I mentioned in Chapter Two, was once a guest on my podcast. When I asked him how he first entered multifamily real estate investing, he shared his story with me.

He began his career as an IT consultant. One day, while on the job with an outside client at his location, the company announced a massive company layoff. He spoke with exiting employees who had served the company for years. They told him they felt helpless and betrayed. They didn't know what they were going to do next or how they would be able to provide for their families.

This experience had a major impact on Venkat. He decided he never wanted to personally go through this and became determined to avoid empowering his employer to kick him to the curb at a moment's notice. This inspired

The Ability to Create Wealth

Venkat to search for another way. He found it in multi-family investing and has not looked back since.

If you have ever been let go or know someone close to you who has endured the experience, you understand the heartache it can bring. A good portion of our identities come from what we do in our jobs. When it is stripped away, we feel demoralized, weak, and aimless. What may have seemed like stability and security at first never existed in the long term. There are never any guarantees. When you are an at-will employee, one day you have a job and the next day you don't.

I've personally experienced being in a company when the hammer came down and people were laid off. I watched the entire office fill with fear and uncertainty, including for those who remained off the chopping block—at least for the time being. Every day after that it crossed everyone's mind that he or she might be axed in the next round.

Here's the harsh reality. Unless you are fortunate and sent off with a golden parachute with some sort of financial package, you lose income the day your employment has ceased. You are left with zero value to sell, except for whatever experience and contacts you might have gained.

WHAT THE WEALTHY KNOW

Wealthy people teach their kids to always have multiple streams of income. Since most of us are not born independently rich, we must find jobs to pay the bills and gain marketable skills. Once employed, we must start saving—even a little at a time, until we have solid footing—so we can *smartly invest*.

However, most people spend money as quickly as they earn it and save little, if anything at all. There are those who allocate 10–20 percent and squirrel it away in a savings account, bonds, or the stock market and *hope* by some form of magic that it will grow into a nest egg. When the bonus, raise, or some other amount of new capital appears, the money gets spent on a bigger house, a fancy car, an exotic vacation, expensive dinners out, jewelry, country club memberships, and so on.

By contrast, the people who started with next to nothing and ended up wealthy were the ones who sacrificed to provide better futures for themselves and their families. They didn't spend the bonus or raise right away, but instead, figured out how to invest in the right opportunities that would build wealth down the road.

I told my kids they should work for a company for a while, learn the business, and then start one of their own. When you become a business owner, you are building something that will have value at a later point in time. Yes, there will be ups and downs along the way. But you will enjoy your freedom and independence, learn from your mistakes, get your bearings, and find the niche that will gradually build wealth.

Allow me to clarify one thing: I believe the goal is to establish multiple income streams *over time*. I also believe you should only focus on tasks related to your strengths and hand off your weaknesses by either hiring someone or outsourcing. Focus on becoming an expert in *one thing* and then add on the next stream of income. Attempting to add multiple streams of income all at once is a recipe for disaster. Become exceptional at this one thing and then layer the next stream on top. It's amazing the golden ideas you come up with when you stick with your primary strengths.

TURN TAXES INTO AN ALLY

Let's come back to the subject of taxes. As I mentioned earlier in this chapter, W-2 employees are taxed at the highest tax rates out there.

When you are taxed through your own business, however, you are entitled to deduct business expenses to calculate profit. This net profit ends up being taxed, but it is at a lower rate than individuals with W-2 jobs.

Now let's discuss how taxes work for real estate investors. The tax code allows real estate investors to deduct depreciation expenses—how much a property has declined in value over time. This is a non-cash expense. Essentially, you own an asset—i.e., a piece of real estate—which may be appreciating in value over time, but the tax code allows you to record expenses for depreciation. This concept involves allocating the cost of a physical asset over its useful life. The beauty of real estate is that the property owner depreciates the property for tax purposes during the hold period. Meanwhile, over the long term, real estate typically is an *appreciating* asset.

Years ago, when I worked for ABN AMRO Bank in the loan trading capital markets group, I was shocked by a certain investor's tax return. The individual had a net worth of $20 million and his bottom-line liability was in the neighborhood of $20,000. While this blew me away, I didn't try to figure out how to do this myself at the time. Shame on me. It wasn't until many years later that I finally took action and learned how to invest properly.

My advice to you: *Do not waste another moment.* You need to take control of your money *right now*. This doesn't mean handing everything over to Wall Street or to a financial advisor and then forgetting about it. Take the time to assess all your options and determine which ones are in your best interests to grow wealth. The thing to know about third parties is that they only have certain products they can offer to you, so that's where they will steer your money.

Always keep in mind: It's *your* money, not theirs. It's time to take responsibility for what is rightfully yours. Learn how the wealthy invest and then do it yourself.

At this stage, there are a few things for you to dive in and learn how to do: maximize your risk adjusted returns; use the existing tax code to keep more of your earnings; and understand how to benefit from velocity in relation to your money. Basically, you want to invest, retain as much of the returns as possible based on tax laws, and then reinvest the profit into new investments.

> *To repeat: You must learn to take control and take action with your money.*

THE THREE BENEFITS OF MULTIFAMILY

I've now been in multifamily real estate for several years. I've learned many things along the way and, admittedly, have made my share of mistakes. In the end, all my deals have worked out for the better in one form or another and contributed to long-term wealth. Entering multifamily real estate was the best decision I ever made in business. In the following sections, I will cover what I view as its three major benefits: *necessity*, *leverage*, and *tax efficiency*.

Necessity

Everyone needs a roof over his or her head—a place to live. I'm going to throw some important numbers related to home ownership at you. Owning a home typically requires a down payment of 20 percent of its price. As of January 2021, the median home price in the United States was $270,000, which translates to a $54,000 down payment. Meanwhile, approximately 64–68 percent of Americans own their own homes; the remainder rent a home or apartment. The United States census counts 121 million households, so let's do some back of the napkin math. If 32–36 percent of these households rent, that would amount to 39–44 million household renters.

Below are a few reasons why an increasing number of people choose to rent over buy:

- Millennials don't seem interested in buying a home. They like the flexibility of being able to move wherever they like at any time.
- Baby boomers are selling their large homes in favor of choosing to rent.
- With skyrocketing housing prices, many people can't afford the cost of buying a home.

For the reasons above and several others, multifamily is a solid risk-adjusted investment. I believe it is a great way to preserve capital and grow it responsibly.

Leverage

When a multifamily property is purchased, the buyer typically receives a loan in the range of 65–80 percent of its value. The remaining 20–35 percent—plus any rehab dollars—are raised with private equity. When the property appreciates in value and is sold, all the profit goes to the equity owners—not the lender. This is where outsized returns may occur.

Let's walk through an example: A multifamily property is purchased for $10 million. The buyer takes out a loan for 70 percent or $7 million. The buying group raises an additional $1 million for rehab. In this scenario, the equity owners have invested $4 million ($3 million for the down payment and $1 million for rehab). Let's suppose the property is held for three to five years and the valuation increases to $15 million. After the $7 million loan is repaid, there is $8 million remaining.

In the above example, the property appreciated by 50 percent, but the limited partner equity owners received 100 percent return (i.e., double their money). This occurred because there is *leverage* on the deal. The equity owners are receiving returns on the entire value of the property—including the loan value—rather than just earning a return on the equity percentage of the deal.

Let's compare this to buying stock, where a similar return rarely happens. If you were to buy $100,000 worth of Amazon stock, the price of Amazon itself would have to double in order to earn twice your investment.

Tax Efficiency

Depreciation expense is powerful when it comes to returns. The property generates a profit and loss statement, just like any other business. The revenue is generated by rent, while expenses are things such as payroll, utilities, property taxes, and repairs. The bottom line is profit or loss. The difference when it comes to real estate is the additional expense of *depreciation*. As mentioned earlier, this is a non-cash expense. In many instances, when depreciation expense is recorded, the property P&L expense results in a loss, which is allocated to the equity owners based on their ownership interest. Many times, this loss is greater than any cash distributions, so an equity owner can receive actual cash distributions throughout the year yet still show a loss for tax purposes. Here, the investors are not liable for the taxes for distributions received.

Another way real estate investors will maximize existing tax laws is by using *bonus depreciation*. Based on the 2017 tax law, this allows for significant depreciation expense in the year of acquisition. This expense often results in approximately 30 percent of the value of the purchased property.

There is another important term to know: *depreciation recapture*. When this recapture is applied, the investor often ends up with a capital gain that is taxable. One of the ways taxpayers avoid paying capital gains is by timing new investments to coincide with the sale of existing investments. Here's a simplified way of looking at this: When an investor sells a property for a gain, he or she will look for new investments that will generate tax losses to cover the gain.

THE MORAL OF THE STORY

Throughout this chapter, I've laid out a few important things to know if you are seeking to build wealth. These are just a few of the summarizing principles to follow:

- Look to increase your number of revenue streams. Do not rely solely on W-2 income.
- Buy assets—ideally, ones that are cash-flowing.
- Build a business that has value that you can possibly sell down the road.
- Take control of your finances. Never just hand your money over to someone to invest for you without understanding where it is going and without having a strong say.
- Understand that not all investments are treated the same in terms of taxes.

Additionally, at the risk of my being redundant: Always learn from others who have knowledge and have "been there, done that"; and take action before opportunities are missed or too many years have slipped by.

If you are considering an area to enter, multifamily investing offers excellent opportunities for building long-term wealth. My business journey can serve as a prime example of how to be proactive and take charge of your money. My wealth grew exponentially in multifamily compared to what I earned when I invested in stocks, ETFs, IRAs, and 401(k) plans. Of course, multifamily is not your only option. You might start some other type of business associated with a strong interest or passion. Or perhaps you'll become an angel investor and help other small businesses. Whatever you decide to do, it's imperative that you take total control of your investment dollars. You must be accountable for growing your own wealth. You will be glad you did every time you review your statements and portfolios.

NINE

Stronger Together

Do you think it is scary to reach out to someone for help? Are you sometimes too intimidated to reach out to others who have greater knowledge and experience than you?

Whether or not you take the initiative and reach out to experts in your field to fill in knowledge gaps all comes down to one thing: conquering a fear of rejection. You wonder whether the person will reject you, assuming he or she even responds to you at all.

I tell my kids, as well as everyone I counsel, that they are guaranteed to face rejection at some point in their lives. You never know how a person will react if you don't try. Failing to reach out to someone is like automatically admitting defeat.

You must always push past the fear of rejection because, if you remain determined and persistent, you will ultimately get to *yes*. You may not receive a positive response on the first try—or even with the individual who is at the top of your list—but, eventually, you will get the answers you need. Your incentive to keep charging ahead to break through your fear is picturing what your next level looks like.

Everyone who made it big in any field had one or several key allies along the way who provided mentorship, information, advice, or inspiration to help him or her figure out how to achieve success. Like you, they were probably afraid. However, they didn't let it stop them from creating a network to help them further their goals. They recognized that any objective worth achieving requires breaking through the fear of others to create a powerful support team.

We are all *stronger, together*.

WHAT VALUE DO YOU OFFER?

When you approach someone who has more experience than you, think about that person, not yourself. Consider what you potentially have to offer this individual.

Some people will assist you simply because they enjoy helping like-minded and hungry go-getters. They will want to see you as an up-and-coming entrepreneur who has passion and confidence. If you can demonstrate that you believe wholeheartedly in your path to success, chances are they will want to help you reach your goals. More often than not, successful people want to give back. It's in their DNA. No doubt there are probably a few experts who helped them out in some capacity when they first started out.

In the following sections, I will share some stories involving people who selflessly helped me out in pivotal moments of my life. They all saw some value—even if it was rough—in terms of what I had to offer.

MY HIGH SCHOOL FOOTBALL COACH

Back in high school, I owned a car and had a regular monthly payment, which meant I needed a steady job. Thankfully, I found one working at a local gas station.

Heading into my senior year, I thought about quitting football to increase my hours at the gas station to help even more with my car payments and have money for other things as well. I heard two voices in my head: one was telling me to work hard, get good grades, and make everyone proud; the other was encouraging me to have a good time and party.

One day, Gary Cassells, my coach, called me into his office. He said to me: "Darin, your senior year of high school football will bring you a lifetime of memories and lessons to be learned. There will always be time for having fun, buying cars, and working—but this last year of high school only comes once and can never be replaced."

I followed his advice and stayed on the team. I'm so glad I did and am thankful to him, even though we didn't have a winning season. That final year helped shape who I am. The experiences, team camaraderie, and lessons will stay with me forever. As the coach said, material objects, such as my car, really do come and go. They only bring temporary fulfillment at best. On the other hand, life experiences build character and serve as a foundation to guide you for the rest of your life.

Did I always like and agree with my high school coach? Not really. Hardly any teen athlete ever does. I thank God to have had him in my life and appreciate the fact that he cared enough to share his wisdom with me.

THE LEADER SETS THE TONE

At that time, I ran with two crowds: the jocks and the hardcore partiers. I happened to be the captain of the football team, a title I took seriously as a major responsibility. The captain is the leader and the one who sets the tone for the team, which isn't so easy when your non-jock friends expect you to party all the time.

I learned right away that my coach didn't care about my social life. He expected me to be a leader and serve as a role model for the team. Meanwhile, my teammates looked to me for direction, even if they didn't specifically ask for it.

What did all of this mean for me? Whether it was during practice or in the middle of the game, I had to give *100 percent all the time*—and expect the same standards from my teammates.

The same goes for when you are an adult as well, whether it comes to your work or your family life. When other people see your determination, passion, and belief in accomplishing the team's goals, it inspires them to contribute their best effort. Every team member must be committed to his or her task and work together to succeed.

At one time or another, everyone—from the leader to the entry level worker—has felt that moment when he or she thinks, *Eh—I just don't feel like it today.* Resisting the temptation to not show up or only putting in half the effort can mean the difference between success and failure. If the team sees a leader "phoning in" the work, the team might follow that lead, which has a trickle-down effect throughout the roster. If, in the reverse, a team member slacks off, it's up to the leader to take notice and pump that individual back up. When that doesn't happen, the rest of the team sees that person "get away" with less than 100 percent effort, which becomes like a contagion spreading through the ranks, and there is an even greater likelihood of failure.

Even today, I admit there are times when I'm not in the mood to record another podcast interview or edit an episode. The urge and inspiration just aren't there, and I think about how I'd much rather head to the golf course instead.

How do I break through a lull like this? I think about an in-person presentation I once attended with bestselling author Brian Tracy. He said something along the lines of: "I write on vacation. I write when I travel. I write on my birthday. *I write every day. . . .*"

At this stage of Tracy's illustrious career, does he *need* to write every single day? Probably not. But he created a winning habit for himself: writing every single day, whether he feels like it or not or is up to the challenge. Who benefits from his diligence? *We* do! His readers. We wouldn't have Brian Tracy's remarkable collection of books to guide us if he weren't so conscientious and dedicated.

It doesn't matter if you are an athlete, a professional writer, or a business professional, you need to set the tone for yourself. Do the things you are meant to do *every single day*. It's the only way to reach the highest level of achievement and enable others to follow your lead.

PEOPLE ABROAD

After working at PriceWaterhouse for two years, I felt an itch to travel the world. I accepted a position with PepsiCo and mapped out some plans involving spending one month in another country, returning home for a week, and then venturing out again for another four weeks. My travels ultimately included Brazil, Peru, Poland, France, Austria, Russia, India, Dubai, and China.

I cherish my time abroad and have many great memories of my travels, but one thing stands out: how the people in these countries were always so accommodating to my travel companions and me. They went out of their way to introduce us to their respective cultures and show us a good time.

My life experiences leave me with several conclusions about the types of people out there:

- There are great people everywhere in the world. You need to seek them out.
- People genuinely want to help one another.
- Build strong teams. We are stronger together!

Great Team

During my first week in Brazil, my colleagues and I went out for dinner and drinks with clients from a local company. To my surprise, they invited people from all levels of their business: receptionists, salespeople, accountants, C-level executives, and everyone in between. It didn't feel like a hierarchy. They were a *team*. Each person was valued for his or her contribution and they worked and communicated seamlessly together. They seemed to genuinely enjoy each other's company. I couldn't have been more impressed by how the C-level executives treated everyone equally and with respect. It didn't matter that they made more money or had fancier offices; in their eyes, they didn't hold themselves up as being any better than their workers. They were *stronger together*.

Crazy Fans

While in São Paulo, Brazil, I also had the opportunity to attend my first live football (soccer) match with colleagues and a few locals. It was a heated display between two hardcore rivals: São Paulo versus Rio. My group and I had been forewarned that these games could get pretty intense—perhaps even dangerous—which turned out to be a spot-on description. The stadium roared and rocked throughout the entire match. A fan for the Rio team had the shirt ripped off his back by a group of opposing fans. In one section of the stands, some fans lit their seats on fire. When the match ended with São Paulo as the victor, the crowd went completely over the edge. I thought the shaking stadium was going to collapse from the stomping and noise.

That was just the start of it. My group and I were thrust out of the stadium by the surging, riled up crowd. We were shoved side-to-side and had no control over where we were going. Once outside, some officers on horseback fruitlessly tried to contain the mob; there were just too many wild and crazy people.

The locals who had joined us for the game had cool heads and knew that my group—meaning, the Americans—were fish out of water and didn't know how to handle the situation. They told us to grab hold of each other and do our best to form a line, so we wouldn't be separated. They knew exactly where to go—and, more importantly, where *not* to go. Thanks to these amazing people, we navigated our way through the mob and safely returned to our hotel.

This became an instant lesson for me. When you have an experienced, capable team by your side, you have each other's backs and can accomplish anything. You also have a fun story to share when it's all over.

BOOK CONTACTS

I've never written a book—until now, that is. At first this was a frightening concept to me. So, what did I do? I gained some strength and confidence about what to do next by attending one of Greg Reid's Secret Knock events. I saw how Greg had published so many books—several of which were bestsellers—and sought out working with his ghostwriter, Gary Krebs, who could help me navigate uncharted waters. I hired him to help me craft the book you are currently holding. Similar to my experience working with Juergen, Gary provided much-needed advice and guidance. I am thankful for his help and guidance along the way.

If you have any interest in becoming an author, make sure you speak with people who have been successful doing it. Better yet, work with people (like Gary) who have not only written books but also worked in traditional publishing houses. Don't try to do it yourself because you don't know what you don't know and could end up making an amateurish mistake. It's kind of like reading a manual on how to be a pilot and thinking you can hop into the cockpit and fly up to the clouds on your own. What do you think would happen?

As you can see, no matter what you hope to achieve, there are people out there who are willing and able to help you, as long as you demonstrate some value to them. If you want to take it to the next level, join a Mastermind consisting of members who know more than you on certain topics and can help you work out ideas, share leads, and problem-solve. The Mastermind concept, which was created by Napoleon Hill (introduced in his book *The Law of Success* and explored more fully in *Think and Grow Rich*), has survived the test of time—nearly a century in fact—and is worth exploring, if only for networking purposes.

Now you are probably asking: *What do I do next?* It's simple: Get out there, take a chance, build a team, and become the successful person the Big Man upstairs created you to be!

TEN

Taking Action

This final chapter, "Taking Action," is extremely important! The difference is that none of the other nine chapters would be possible to accomplish without this final summarizing message which, if you've been reading carefully, has been mentioned in some way in virtually every chapter.

Dreams are wonderful things to have, and you want to have passion to fuel your engine. However, the most successful entrepreneurs establish goals and an action plan that can facilitate achieving those goals and fulfilling those dreams. Dr. Greg S. Reid famously said, "A dream written down becomes a goal. A goal broken down into steps becomes a plan. A plan backed by action makes your dreams reality."

Think about the people who have successfully lost weight and kept it off. What is the difference between them and the many who repeatedly fail? Everyone who diets wants to lose weight. They may dream about it. They may also have a heartfelt passion for it. But do they set firm goals and create a solid action plan that will lead to sustainable results? For all the diet books and diet plans out there, the secret to weight loss is always going to be the same: eat better, exercise, and be patient as you stay the course.

In other words, *put in the work*. Focus on your dream and achieving your vision *every single day*. If you are performing an activity that doesn't help accomplish a goal or fulfill your dream in some way, you are probably doing something wrong.

There may be occasions when you must take action, even though you don't have 100 percent of the information. It's simply not possible to always have every piece of data necessary at your fingertips, despite exhaustive research. On these occasions, you must make a decision one way or the other. A lot of people make decisions by *not deciding* or putting them off for so long that the deadline is missed, and the call ends up being made for you.

Indecision is never going to broaden your learning or grow your business. When you allow things to happen by chance—usually out of fear—you are allowing others to make the decision for you, which sacrifices your ability to control a given scenario. It also becomes a sign of weakness to others.

Now ask yourself the following: *What things can I cut out of my day that wouldn't make a shred of difference in terms of making my dreams come true?* Question everything you do and deprioritize—or even drop—the tasks that don't further your lifelong aspirations.

One day, you'll look back on the journey you have undertaken and take stock of everything you've accomplished. Did this success happen overnight? Of course not, although it may seem that way to an outsider.

This is when other people will be seeking *you* out to provide counsel. They'll ask, "Can you teach me how to do it?" Suddenly, you'll realize how much knowledge and experience you've gained over the years—a great deal of which came from other experts—and now it's time for you to give back.

At the same time, no matter how much success you achieve, always continue to explore, learn, and grow. Try to avoid being stagnant and staying in the same place. The world is simply too volatile to sit back and let things ride and hope things will stay the same. If you do, the world will progressively change and leave you behind.

Whether you continue to pursue your dreams in real estate or in another endeavor, I wish you the best of success. Now—go out there and take action to build wealth!

CLOSING THOUGHTS

In this closing section, I would like to share some new goals and desires that I would like to learn about and pursue. I share this information to hold myself accountable and to show you, the reader, that there is always another fresh and exciting dream to chase. To accomplish a new goal, there will always be challenges that take us out of our comfort zones. Remember: These are opportunities to stretch and grow!

1. I want to learn about and invest in crypto.
2. I want to travel across the United States with my wife, either in some type of RV or through Airbnb.
3. I want to learn about angel investing.

There you have it. The above list makes me uncomfortable because I don't (as of yet) have expertise in these areas. I am excited to take the time and learn about them—and then take action!

SUGGESTED READING

These books have inspired me on my journey. No matter where you may be on yours, I think they are worth checking out.

Brunson, Russell. *Dotcom Secrets*. Hay House, 2022 (paperback).
Brunson, Russell. *Expert Secrets*. Hay House, 2022 (paperback).
Brunson, Russell. *Traffic Secrets*. Hay House, 2020.
Coelho, Paulo. *The Alchemist: 25th Anniversary Edition*. HarperOne, 2014.
Covey, Stephen R. *The 7 Habits of Highly Effective People: 25th Anniversary Edition*. Simon & Schuster, 2020.
Dalio, Ray. *Principles for Dealing with the Changing World Order*. Simon & Schuster, 2021.
Dalio, Ray. *Principles: Life and Work*. Simon & Schuster, 2017.
DeMarco, M. J. *The Millionaire Fastlane*. Viperion Publishing, 2011.

Duhigg, Charles. *The Power of Habit*. Random House, 2014.

Eves, Derral. *The YouTube Formula*. Wiley, 2021.

Fairless, Joe. *The Best Ever Apartment Syndication Book*. Theo Hicks, 2018.

Ferriss, Tim. *The 4-Hour Workweek*. Ebury Press, 2011.

Ferriss, Tim. *Tools of Titans*. Penguin Random House, 2016.

Gunderson, Garrett B., with Stephen Palmer. *Killing Sacred Cows*. Greenleaf, 2008.

Hardy, Darren. *The Compound Effect*. Monjul Publishing, 2021.

Hill, Napoleon. *Think and Grow Rich*. Sound Wisdom, 2019. First published in 1937.

Itzler, Jesse. *Living with a Seal*. Center Street, 2016.

Jones, Carson. *Subscribe, Rate & Review*. Self-published, 2019.

Kiyosaki, Robert T. *Rich Dad, Poor Dad*. Plata Publishing, 2017.

Kiyosaki, Robert. *Rich Dad's Cashflow Quadrant*. Plata Publishing, 2011.

Klaff, Oren. *Pitch Anything*. McGraw-Hill, 2011.

Lechter, Sharon L., and Dr. Greg S. Reid. *Three Feet from Gold*. Sound Wisdom, 2020.

McConaughey, Matthew. *Greenlights*. Headline, 2021.
Olson, Jeff. *The Slight Edge: Turning Simple Disciplines into Massive Success and Happiness.* Greenleaf, 2013.
Reid, Dr. Greg S., with Gary M. Krebs. *Wealth Made Easy.* BenBella, 2019.
Schwartz, David J., PhD. *The Magic of Thinking Big*. Simon & Schuster, 1987.
Sinek, Simon. *Start With Why.* Portfolio, 2011.
Stenziano, Jake, and Gino Barbaro. *The Honey Bee*. River Grove Books, 2019.
Sullivan, Dan. *Who Not How*. Hay House, 2020.
Tanner, Andy. *401(k)aos.* Tanner Training, 2012.
Thompson, Hunter. *Raising Capital for Real Estate*. Independently published, 2019.
Tracy, Brian. *Eat That Frog!, 3rd Edition.* Berrett-Koehler Publishers, 2017.
Tracy, Brian. *Maximum Achievement*. Simon & Schuster, 1995.
Voss, Chris, with Tahl Raz. *Never Split the Difference*. HarperBusiness, 2016.
Wheelwright, Tom. *Tax-Free Wealth.* BZK Press, 2018.
Zell, Sam. *Am I Being Too Subtle?* Portfolio, 2017.

ABOUT THE AUTHOR

Darin Batchelder started as a CPA with PriceWaterhouse and PepsiCo. He transitioned into sales, selling software applications for several technology companies. He then worked in the institutional loan trading industry with ABN AMRO, an international bank based in the Netherlands, with a main focus on trading jumbo residential portfolios and multifamily portfolios bank to bank. In 2007, he founded TZK Capital, focused on trading clean credit performing loans to include residential, multifamily, and commercial real estate loans bank to bank. He has since traded in excess of $4 billion in loans.

Darin began purchasing real estate in the fourth quarter of 2017 with a new construction duplex. At the beginning of 2018, he started to invest passively into other sponsors' multifamily deals. He closed his first lead sponsor deal—a 76-unit townhome community—at the end of 2018. In a brief period of time, he has now invested in a total of 4,000 multifamily units.

Darin, who has a son and daughter, lives in the Dallas–Fort-Worth area with his wife, Tiffany.

To learn more about Darin Batchelder and contact him:

Website: https://darinbatchelder.com/

Instagram: @batchelderdarin

Facebook (Meta): https://www.facebook.com/batchelderdarin/

LinkedIn: https://www.linkedin.com/in/darin-batchelder-8855b620/

DARIN BATCHELDER'S PODCAST

Check out Darin Batchelder's Podcast!

On the show, you will learn how to grow your wealth through multifamily real estate investing, be introduced to the players who are getting it done, and learn how you can get involved!

Sign up at https://darinbatchelder.com/ to receive free weekly updates.

FREE 5-STEP PROCESS TO PASSIVELY INVESTING IN REAL ESTATE

Are you interested in learning how to passively invest in real estate?

Visit our website at https://darinbatchelder.com to download your free copy of my 5-Step Process for Passively Investing in Real Estate.

www.ingramcontent.com/pod-product-compliance
Lightning Source LLC
Chambersburg PA
CBHW050416120526
44590CB00015B/1990